THE THREEFOLD SECRET OF THE HOLY SPIRIT

by

James H. McConkey

MOODY PRESS
CHICAGO

Copyright 1897, by James H. McConkey

*This edition published by
permission of the
Silver Publishing Society,
Pittsburgh, Pa*

More than 575,000 published previously.
Translated into 20 languages

Printed in the U.S.A.

THE THREEFOLD SECRET
OF THE HOLY SPIRIT

Contents

	Page
1. The Secret of His Incoming	
The Abundant Life	9
The Secret of His Incoming	22
2. The Secret of His Fullness	
The Secret of His Fullness	45
Trust	59
Manifestation	72
My Consecration	85
3. The Secret of His Constant Manifestation	
Abiding In Christ	89
Abiding in Christ	89

Note: The "Revised Version" or "R.V." referred to by the author is the British revision of 1885, upon which the American Standard Version of 1901 is based.

I

THE SECRET OF HIS INCOMING

Union With Christ

This Jesus . . . having received of the Father the promise of the Holy Ghost.   Acts 2:32, 33.

But of Him are ye in Christ Jesus.   I Cor. 1:30.

In whom . . . ye were sealed with the Holy Spirit of promise.   Eph. 1:13, R. V.

The Abundant Life

"I am come that they might have life, and that they might have it *more abundantly*" (John 10:10).

* * * * *

AS THE WEST-BOUND TRAVELER speeds over the Alleghenies, his watchful gaze can hardly fail to note the gleaming surface of a little artificial lake whose azure-tinted waters mirroring the skies above, add much to the beauty of the great railroad system which spans our native state. This lakelet, embosomed in the depths of the mountains, is the reservoir which furnishes water to a busy neighboring city, and is fed by a mountain stream of modest supply. In the drought of last summer the infilling streams dwindled to a tiny thread; the waters of the reservoir sank to their lowest limits; and all the ills of a protracted water famine, with its constant menace to health and home, beset the city. The most rigid economy was urged by the authorities; the water was cut off save for a few hours per day; and the scant supply of precious fluid was carefully husbanded against emergencies. Not a hundred miles from this city lies a smaller lake nestling also among the mountains. In its very center bursts forth a natural fountain of unlimited abundance and marvelous beauty. In the same summer of disastrous drought this famous spring without abating one jot of its wondrous flow or sinking one inch below the lip of its encircling embankment, furnished the thirsty city with fullest supply and then still outflowed over its waste-weir a sparkling, leaping stream of unstinted copiousness, earning right royally the privilege not only of refreshing with its water, but of christening with its own name the city of "The Beautiful Fountain." The larger city in truth had water. But the smaller one had it "more abundantly." The scanty rivulet that trickled into the reservoir was barely enough to save from keen thirst. But the living bubbling fountain, pouring out its liquid wealth in prodigal flow for its native town, had left still enough to slake the thirst of a city many times the size of its greater neighbor.

Even so is it with the life of the Holy Spirit in God's children. Some have His indwelling life only as the trickling stream with scarce enough to keep and refresh them at times of test and stress, and never knowing what His fullness means. Others there are in whom the words of Jesus are joyously fulfilled: "I am come that they might have life, and that they might have it *more abundantly*" (more aboundingly). Not only are they filled with the Spirit in their own inner life, but they overflow in abundant, outgiving blessing to the hungry and thirsty lives about them that seek to know the secret

THE SECRET OF HIS INCOMING

of their refreshing. Sorrow comes, but it cannot rob them of their great peace. Dark grow the days, but their childlike faith abounds more and more. Heavily fall the afflictive blows but like the oil well which, under the blow of the explosive, gives forth a more abundant flow because of the very shattering of its rocky reservoir, so their lives only pour out an ever increasing and enriching volume of blessing upon those about them. An unceasing stream of prayer flows from their hearts. Praise leaps as instinctively and artlessly from their lips as glad song bursts from the soaring skylark. Trust has become a second nature; joy is its natural outcome; and ceaseless service springs not from the bondage of duty but as the gracious response of love. They are not like dry pumps, needing to be aided by others through impoured draughts of exhortation and stimulation ere they will give forth their scant supply. They are rather deep-driven artesian wells, spontaneous, constant, spirit-flowing. In them the Master's words have been fulfilled: "The water which I shall give him shall be in him a well of water springing up into everlasting life."

Such were the lives of the apostles after the eventful day of Pentecost; transformed from timid, self-seeking, hesitating followers to bold, sacrificing, heroic messengers of Jesus Christ; preaching His Gospel with wondrous power, joy, and effectiveness. Such was Stephen, *"full* of faith and the Holy Ghost"; and Barnabas, *"full* of the Holy Ghost and of faith."

12   THE THREEFOLD SECRET OF THE HOLY SPIRIT

The men chosen to wait on tables were *"full* of the Holy Ghost." Paul swept to and fro in his great missionary journeys *"filled* with the Holy Ghost." Such was Charles Finney preaching the word of life with fiery earnestness born of a mighty *fullness* of the Spirit. Such were Edwards, and Moody, and multitudes of others; and such an abundant life as this does God hold out to all His children as their birthright, their lawful inheritance. In His picture of its precious fruitage (Gal. 5:22, 23), we see it to be a life of

Abundant Love

See the apostles filled with burning zeal to give the Gospel of Christ's love to all. Mark Stephen's intense love for souls. Behold Peter's glowing heart and fervent testimonies now well attesting his earnest assertion, "Yea, Lord, thou knowest that I love thee." Mark the man of Tarsus, consumed with such a love for dying men as naught but God could inspire, and none but God could surpass. His great throbbing heart is too small a fountain to contain; his thrilling, burning words too weak a bridge to convey; his weak, toil-spent body too feeble a tabernacle to incarnate all the fullness of his passionate love for souls. So too Brainerd toils, fasts, weeps, and dies for his Indians, because of the divine love within him. Judson is driven from the land of his choice; is baffled again and again in his efforts to obtain a foothold in Burma; languishes in prison amid unspeakable horrors and sufferings, yet the flame of love never abates. Livingstone travels through a pathless wilderness; endures untold hardships; is broken-hearted by the vision of the infamy and anguish of the slave traffic; yet, dying upon his knees in holy prayer, love burns more intensely than in the days of his youth. Paton exiles himself among the cannibals; faces difficulties that would daunt the most daring; labors with patience, prays with mighty faith; suffers with unmurmuring fortitude, reaps with joy unspeakable; and then girdles the earth in his travels, his heart all the while pulsating with the Spirit's own mighty love.

Whose heart has not thrilled at the story of Delia, the sin-marred queen of the Mulberry street dive, and of her rescue from a life of shame? Yet it was the burning love of Christ in her heart which led Mrs. Whittemore to seek to save this lost one. It was love that breathed out the earnest prayer over the spotless rose and offered it to the erring one. It was love that drew the poor girl to the Door of Hope in the hour of her conviction. It was love that welcomed her, wept over her, and melted her heart with contrition and repentance. And then love begat love. For saved to the uttermost, this rescued one broke the alabaster box of her redeemed life as an offering of sweetest savor at the feet of Him whose love had saved her, and went forth to tell the story of that love to others. In prisons, in the slums, in street meetings, wherever this ransomed one told the story of Him who loved us and gave Himself for us, the kindling love of the Holy Ghost so fired her soul that strong, sin-hardened men, bowing and sobbing under her thrilling, impassioned words, were swept by scores into the kingdom of God. For one brief year the love-life of God streamed, brimful through the open channel of her surrendered being; quickening, thrilling and inspiring all with whom she came in touch, and then she went to Him who was the fountain of her life of abounding love.

In an interior city dwells a friend "grappled to our souls with hooks of steel" in the precious bonds of the kinship that is in Christ Jesus. By the grace of God he has been wonderfully saved from a life of scoffing, derisive, soul-destroying infidelity. For days and weeks at a time he will be engaged in the busy, loving ministrations of a secular profession. Then, without warning the Holy Ghost will suddenly lay upon him the burden of lost souls. Driven by the Spirit to the seclusion of his own chamber, the love of God for the lost will so flood his being that for hours at a time he will lie upon his face sobbing out his broken petitions to God for their salvation. Then, going forth into the surrounding country with mighty, convicting messages, from a heart overflowing with the abundant love-life of his Master, he preaches the Gospel of Christ in the needy places. In the few short years since

THE SECRET OF HIS INCOMING 15

his conversion God has given to this devoted servant over six hundred souls as the fruitage of the life of abundant love. Beloved, are we walking in this abounding love-life? Do we know its power, joy and fullness? If not, we are falling short of the high calling of Him who came that we might have love not meagerly, but have it *abundantly*.

Again it is a life of

Abundant Peace

"The fruit of the Spirit is peace" (Gal. 5:22). "*The peace of God* . . . shall keep your hearts and minds" (Phil. 4:7). "My peace I leave with you" (John 14:27).

There rises up here the vision of a lovely midsummer forenoon. As we lay quietly resting, the inside shutters of the window under the puff of a passing breeze suddenly opened. Straightway there lay before our gaze a beautiful picture of a sky of cloudless blue; green hills stretching away in the dim distance; and noble river smiling and tossing its sparkling waves in the broad path of the sunlight. A moment the vision lingered and then, under the fitful gust of a contrary breeze, the shutters suddenly slammed shut. At once all the glory and beauty of the scene vanished, and stayed hidden until another flow of wind again disclosed its loveliness, only to be followed anew by its disappearance.

Even thus, we thought, is the peace of the natural heart. For awhile, when all goes well and plans prosper, our hearts are content and at peace. But let a gust of adverse fortune, a baffling of some favorite purpose befall us, and at once peace vanishes and anxious care broods in its place. Peace indeed we have, but its manifestation is inconstant and fickle, filling us one day with rest, leaving us the next in darkness and hopelessness. What a contrast with this is the peace of the abundant Spirit-life! For there is a peace which "passeth all understanding," and—as one has well said—"all misunderstanding"; a peace which keeps us, not we it; a peace of which it is said, "Thou wilt keep him in perfect peace whose mind is stayed on thee"; a peace which, because born not of an outer calm, but an inner Christ, cannot be disturbed by sting or storm. It is the peace of the fullness of the Spirit. The sea has a surface which tosses, and frets, foams and spumes, rises, staggers, and falls under every passing wind that assails its unstable life. But it has also deeps which have lain in motionless peace for ages, unswept by wind, unswayed by billow. So there are for the timorous heart moveless deeps of peace whose unbroken rest can be pictured only by that wonderful phrase—"the peace of God." *The peace of God!* Think of it for a moment. How wondrous must be *God's* peace! With Him there is no frailty, no error, no sin. With Him there is no past to lament, no future to dread; no blunders, no mistakes to fear;

THE SECRET OF HIS INCOMING

no plans to be thwarted; no purposes to be unmet. No death can overcome, no suffering weaken, no ideal be unfulfilled, no perfection unattained. Past, present or future; vanishing time or endless eternity; life or death, hope or fear, storm or calm—naught of these, and naught else within the bounds of the universe can disturb the peace of Him who calls himself the *God of peace*. And it is this peace that is ours to possess. "*The peace of God* shall keep *your* heart and minds." Not a human peace attained by self-struggle or self-discipline, but divine peace— the very peace which God himself has, yea, is. This is why Jesus Himself says, "My peace I give unto you." Human, man-made peace, which rises and falls with the vicissitudes of life, is worthless; but the peace of *Christ*, what a gift is this! Mark the surroundings when Christ spake these words, and how wonderful this peace appears! It was just before His death. Before Him is the kiss of the traitor; the hiss of the scourge; the weary blood-stained way to death; the hiding of His Father's face; the thorn-crowned, purple-robed mockery of His kingship; and the awful torture-climax of the cross. If ever a man's soul ought to be torn with agony, burdened with horror, surely this is the hour. But instead of gloom, and fear, and shuddering anticipation, hear His wondrous words, "*My peace* I leave with you!" Surely a peace like this is worth having! Surely a peace which does not take flight before such a hideous vision of betrayal, agony, and death is an *abundant* peace; is one of which He can well say, "I leave it with you; it will stay; it is the God-peace which abides forever. My children, behold my hour of crisis, darker than shall ever come to any of you, yet my peace abides without a tremor. My peace has stood the supreme test, therefore it can never fail; I pass it on to you."

Some years ago a friend narrated to us an experience of the Johnstown Flood which we have never forgotten. His home was below that ill-fated city, and when the flood burst he, with others, hurried out upon the bridge, rope in hand, to rescue if possible any unfortunates who might be borne down the river. Presently, as he waited, his attention was attracted by the approach of a half-submerged house which the rushing torrent was bearing swiftly toward him, and upon the roof of which he saw the recumbent form of a woman. With heart thrilling with sympathy and earnest desire to compass her rescue, he quickly made ready, and as the strange craft neared the bridge he cast the rope with eager expectancy, but it fell short of the mark. Rushing to the lower side of the bridge, as the house swept under the arching span, he again cast the rope with feverish haste and intensity, but again it failed of its merciful purpose. "And then," said our friend, "as the last hope of rescue faded with the second failure to reach her, and death became her inevitable doom, the occupant of the roof, who had been reclining on its steep slope with her head resting upon her hand, turned, and a sweet womanly face looked up into mine. Until my dying day I shall never forget the expression upon that upturned countenance! Instead of the fear, horror, and agony with which I expected to see it distorted, it was quiet and calm, with an unspeakable, serene, abiding peace, and with a kindly nod of recognition of my poor effort to save her, as she swept on to certain death that Peace kindled into a glory that 'ne'er was seen on land or sea,' whose radiance was unshadowed even by the awful roar and strife of the elements about." "Ah, friend," thought I, as the tears leaped unbidden to my eyes under this touching story, "she must have been a child of the Lord; she knew Him; and this that kept her was the Peace of God."

Then too it is a life of

ABUNDANT POWER FOR SERVICE

"Ye shall receive *power* when the Holy Ghost is come upon you," said Christ to His disciples. And their lives straightway became a never-ceasing record of mighty deeds done in the power of the Spirit. "Stephen," we are told, "full of faith and *power*, did great wonders and miracles among the people" (Acts 6:8). Charles G. Finney, entering a mill, was so filled with the power of the Spirit that the operatives fell upon their knees in tears before the mere presence of the evangelist, ere he had uttered a word. At a camp-meeting where the most learned and eloquent sermons had utterly failed to move men to repentance, the whole congregation broke down in tears of conviction and penitence under the quiet words of an unassuming man who spoke manifestly filled with the Spirit. A word, a prayer, an earnest appeal, a song that would fall otherwise unheeded, goes home to the heart, filled with some subtle power when issuing from a Spirit-filled life. Moody testifies that never until he knew the fullness of the Spirit did he know the fullness of God's power in his preaching, but after that his preached words never failed of some fruitage Neither is the power of the abundant life confined to the preaching of God's word. God gives to some power in prayer; to others power in testimony; to others power in song; to others power in suffering and affliction. Every soul that knows the Spirit's abounding life is touching other lives with power whose full scope and intensity he will never know until the Lord comes to reward.

Nor is the fullness of the Spirit limited to abundant love, peace, and power. It is a life too of abundant joy; "the joy of the Lord is our strength"; of abundant long-suffering, girding us with patience under trials that we never could otherwise endure; of abundant gentleness, as Christ's own gentleness takes possession of us; of abundant goodness, abundant faith, abundant meekness, abundant self-control. That it is not meant for apostles, or ministers, or missionaries, or teachers only, but for all of God's children is clear, for: "The promise is unto you, and to your children, and to all that are afar off."

What Is Its Secret?

The Secret of His Incoming

How then shall our heart-longings for the fullness of the Spirit be satisfied? How shall we know His abundance of love, peace, joy, and power for service? What is the secret of this abundant life, this fullness of the Spirit?

We answer first, negatively: *It is not that we have not received the Holy Ghost.* Seeing the powerlessness, the barrenness, the lack of love, joy, peace, and power in many Christian lives, and knowing these to be the fruitage of the abundant life of the Spirit, many leap to the conclusion that the Spirit has not been received, else how account for the feeble manifestations of His presence and power? Wherefore the first thing we need clearly to see is that *every child of God has received the gift of the Holy Ghost.* It is of the greatest importance, in the search for the secret of the abundant life, that this glorious fact should be clearly seen and accepted by the believer. For if he has not received the Holy Ghost, then his attitude should be that of waiting, petitioning, and seeking for the gift which is not yet his. But if he *has* received the Holy Ghost, then he must take an entirely different attitude, namely,

THE SECRET OF HIS INCOMING

not of waiting and praying for the Holy Ghost to be received but of yielding and surrendering to Him who has already been received. In the first case *we* are waiting on God to do something; in the other God is waiting on *us* to do something.

It will be seen at once that if a man is occupying either of these attitudes when he ought to be in the other, then confusion and failure are bound to result. For example, the simple conditions of salvation are repentance from sins and faith in the Lord Jesus Christ. Now, to keep a truly penitent soul in the attitude of seeking or praying for forgiveness, instead of simple faith in God's Word that he has been forgiven in Christ, is a ruinous mistake, leading to darkness and agony, instead of the light and joy that God means him to have. On the other hand, to try to get an impenitent soul to "only believe," instead of first repenting of his sins, will keep him in equal darkness, and make his nominal acceptance of Christ a mere profession and hypocrisy. Exactly so is it with the case in hand. If the absence of the abundant life of the Spirit in us is due, as we are persuaded it is, not to the fact that He has not come in, but that we have not surrendered to Him who is *already* in, then it is a tremendous and fatal mistake to keep a soul waiting and seeking, instead of surrendering and yielding. It puts him at cross purposes with God. He keeps calling on God to give the Holy Ghost, to baptize him with the Spirit. But

God has already done this to all who are in Christ, and is calling on him to fulfill certain conditions by which he may know the abundance of the Spirit, not the Spirit who is to come, but the Spirit who is already in him. Have we not known His children to wait, and cry, and agonize for the gift of the Holy Ghost through long, weary days, months, and even years, from not knowing the truth of His Word upon this point? For it is "the truth that makes us free," and if we know it not we cannot be free. That all we, then, who are God's children, have "received the Holy Spirit," the "gift of the Holy Spirit," (as God uses that term) is clearly taught in His Word, for

1. *We have fulfilled the conditions of the gift of the Holy Ghost.* What are these conditions? We would expect them first to be very simple and easily comprehended by the most unlearned. God does not, and would not, make the greatest gift of His love to us, next to that of His Son, to hinge upon any but the very simplest and plainest conditions. Through all the ages the great promise of the Spirit was in the divine mind preparing for fulfillment. He would not have a single child of His to miss the way. He has made it a great highway, and set up fingerboards so plain and unambiguous that only preconceived human opinions, doctrines, theories, theologies, and darkening of counsel could make us miss it so grievously as we have done. Moreover when we have endeavored to lay aside our own

THE SECRET OF HIS INCOMING

opinions and prejudices, and to seek the light of His Word alone, we have complicated the question by confining ourselves almost entirely to the experience of the apostles at the day of Pentecost. Accepting this as the "pattern in the mount" for us, we, consciously or unconsciously, deem the same conditions needful. Right here note that in our search for the conditions of the gift of the Holy Ghost we have confined ourselves too closely to the apostolic *experience* instead of the apostolic *teaching*, at Pentecost. Now a man's experience of conversion may be most marvelous and impressive in its accompaniments. But many a man who has had a genuine, glorious experience of conversion utterly fails when he tries to lead others to Christ. Why? *Because he imparts into his directions to the anxious seeker conditions from his own experience which are not essential scriptural conditions for others.* Equally disastrous has been this practice in the teaching concerning the glorious truths of the Spirit, and that too, by men who have had genuine, striking experiences of His fullness of blessing. They teach us to pray without ceasing to wait not only ten days but ten years if need be; to "wait for the promise of the Comforter," to look for wonderful experiences, etc. How many an anxious soul has thus been plunged into hopeless confusion and spiritual darkness! The trouble is the same. They are endeavoring to guide us solely by the apostolic *experience* instead of the apostolic *teaching*. But the former is much more difficult of analysis than the latter, and it may be fairly said to be abnormal to us in these important respects, that, the apostles lived before Christ came, while He walked the earth, and after He left it. They thus had one experience of the Holy Ghost as Old Testament believers; another when the risen Christ breathed upon them and said "receive ye the Holy Ghost"; another when the ascended Christ poured out the Holy Ghost upon them, at Pentecost. But this is not true of us. To our mind, the important question is not so much how the apostles—who lived through dispensations, loosely speaking, of Father, Son, and Holy Spirit—received the Holy Spirit, as how men who lived in the latter, *as we do*, received Him. The experience that matches ours is not so much that of the apostles, who had also believed on Jesus before the gift of the Holy Ghost, as that of the apostles' converts who believed on Him exactly as we do, after the work of Christ was finished, and after the Holy Ghost was given. Let us therefore now ask not so much what did the apostles *experience* as what did they *teach*. Not only how did they receive the Holy Ghost, but how did they instruct others to receive Him. And here, as always, we find the Word of God wondrously simple, if we will lay aside our own prejudgments and hear only what it says. For on that same Pentecostal day the apostolic teaching was just as clear as the apostolic experience was wonderful.

THE SECRET OF HIS INCOMING

If ever there was a time when the presence of God filled a human body, burned in a human heart, and inspired human lips with errorless accuracy of teaching, surely it was when Peter preached his great sermon on the Day of Pentecost. All aflame he was with the mighty anointing of power, and it was the God of truth Himself who spoke through him and answered the pleading cry of the multitude, "What shall we do," by His own divine word of direction and teaching. And what does He say? "Then Peter said unto them, Repent and be baptized every one of you in the name of Jesus Christ for the remission of sins, and ye shall receive the gift of the Holy Ghost" (Acts 2:38).

It is evident from many passages in the Word that baptism was here an ordinance administered upon faith in Christ as a sin-bearer, and thus God here taught through Peter this great truth: The two great conditions of receiving the Holy Ghost are *repentance,* and *faith in Christ for the remission of sins.* No other conditions are required. Repent of your sins, believe in the Lord Jesus Christ for the remission of your sins (being baptized thereupon), and "ye shall receive the gift of the Holy Ghost." There are two things for us to do, and then one thing God does. If you do these two things, you *shall receive,* says God. The promise is absolute. Surely man has no right to put any other requirement between the "Repent and believe," and the "Ye shall receive," since God Himself puts none. If any soul honestly repents and believes on the Lord Jesus Christ for the remission of his sins, then the heavens would fall before God would fail to fulfill His promise, "Ye shall receive."

Therefore the only question that the child of God, in doubt whether he has received the gift of the Holy Ghost, need ask is: Have I turned away from my sins with an honest heart, and am I trusting, not in my own poor works, but in Jesus Christ as my sin-bearer and Saviour? If so God has given me the Holy Ghost, and the peace I find in my heart is born alone of that Spirit whom "if any man have not he is none of His." If we have never honestly repented, or have never simply believed in Jesus Christ, then we have not received the Spirit. But if we have fulfilled these two simple conditions—a fact easily known to ourselves—then God must have given us His great gift. Nevertheless He does not leave us to rest alone upon logic even as good as this, but buttresses it with the next great proof that we have so received Him, namely:

2. *By the witness of the Spirit Himself; by our own experience of His incoming, when we fulfilled these conditions.* "Therefore being justified by faith we have peace with God through our Lord Jesus Christ." Do not many of us remember the very day and hour and place, when having repented and believed in Jesus Christ, our hearts were filled with

wondrous peace and joy? Or even if it did to others of us come less definitely as to time and place, yet was the experience of the peace that came into our heart, to replace the distress and unrest that had dwelt there for years, any the less definite or wonderful because it had stolen upon us gradually and quietly? The Spirit bore witness with our spirit. No power in existence could bring the peace that we have concerning past sins save the Holy Ghost. Jesus alone is our peace concerning the past, and the Holy Ghost alone could communicate to our hearts the experience of that peace. The fact that it is there is proof absolute of the Spirit's presence. Let none rob us of this conscious attestation of His incoming. We know He is in us because none but Him could work in us such fruitage as that of which we are conscious. We repented; we believed; and He came in, to "abide with us forever." Let our hearts be at rest. Nor does it matter much that this is not what *we* mean by "the gift of the Holy Ghost." It is what *God says*. And the sooner we use God's terms, accept God's statements, and obey God's commands, the sooner will the darkness that shrouds this great truth flee away and let in upon our souls the clear shining of the day.

3. *It is the constant assertion of God's Word concerning believers.* Notice how emphatic this is. "Know ye not that ye *are* the temple of God and the Spirit of God *dwelleth* in you?" (I Cor. 3:16). Not

that we *shall* be hereafter, but that *now* we believers *are* the temple of God, and that the Spirit *dwells* now (present tense) in us. Again (mark the tense) "What! know ye not that your body *is* the temple of the Holy Ghost which *is* in *you,* which ye *have* of God" (I Cor. 6:19). Again "For *ye are* the temple of the living God" (II Cor. 6:16). Also "Try your own selves, whether ye are in the faith; prove your own selves. Or know ye not as to your own selves that Jesus Christ is in you? unless indeed ye be reprobate" (II Cor. 13:5 R.V.). How clear this last passage is upon the points named! Note the simple condition again: "Try your own selves whether *ye are in the faith.*" That is, are you believers? Are you simply trusting the Lord Jesus Christ for salvation? If so, "Know ye not as to your own selves that *Jesus Christ is in you?*" Unless indeed when you examine yourself you find that you are "reprobate," that is, "not-standing-the-test," not trusting Christ, but something else. How simple all this is, and how harmonious, with the truth as Peter preached it! He says, "Repent and believe in Jesus Christ." And Paul says to these who have repented and are now believers, "Don't you know that the only question you have to ask yourselves is: 'Am I trusting in Christ?' If so Jesus dwells in you, in the Holy Ghost." Beloved, even though we had never had a single emotional experience of the indwelling presence of the Holy Ghost yet we would be bold indeed—to say nothing worse—to deny the glorious fact of His indwelling

THE SECRET OF HIS INCOMING

in the face of the constant, explicit, assertions of God that *we are* His temple, that *he does* dwell *in us* and that we *have* this great gift of the Spirit from God *now*.

4. *Christ and the Apostles always take this truth for granted in addressing believers.* Note Paul's exclamation of surprise that they should for a moment lose sight of this fundamental truth. *"What! Know ye not?"* (I Cor. 6:19). Are ye ignorant or forgetful of this great and glorious truth that the Holy Ghost dwelleth in you? (I Cor. 3:16). Do you grow doubtful of His presence because you are not having any such wonderful experience of it as you expect? Do you forget that His indwelling does not depend upon your emotions, but upon your *union with Christ* which has been long since accomplished by *God* through your faith in Him? (I Cor. 1:30). And then again (Acts 19:2). He says to them not "Have ye received the Holy Ghost since ye believed?" as in the Authorized Version, but "Did ye receive the Holy Ghost *when* ye believed?" showing that he expected all the children of God to receive the gift at the time of repentance and belief in Christ.

So too, notice Christ's attitude toward the same truth in His constant use of the word, "Abide." "Abide in me and I in you." "If ye abide in me." "And now, little children, abide in him" (I John 2:28). What is the truth here? Clearly this: The word, "abide," means to stay, to remain in a place in which you already are. Thus, when you request a company of people to abide, to stay in a room, we at once understand that those addressed are already there. When Paul said, "Except these abide in the ship ye can not be saved," we know that they were already in the ship. Now Christ's word to the sinner is, "Come," because he is out of Christ. But His word to the believer is, "Abide, stay," because he is already, and forever, *in* Christ. But no man can be in Christ and not have received the Holy Ghost. It is impossible. For He is the giver of the Spirit. In Him *is* life and the instant we are united to Him by faith we must receive the Spirit. The wire can no more be joined to the dynamo and not receive the electric fluid; the branch can no more be joined to the vine and not receive the thrill of life, than we can be joined to Christ by faith and not receive His great resurrection gift. "I am the vine, ye are the branches."

But someone now says: "I believe that it is the Holy Ghost who has regenerated me, and that I could not be born again except by His agency. But I do not believe this is what God means by receiving the gift of the Holy Ghost. Is there not a second experience for the believer in which, *after* his conversion, he receives the Holy Ghost for service in great power and abundance, such as he has never known before? Did not Paul say to the Ephesian converts: 'Have ye received the Holy Ghost *since*

THE SECRET OF HIS INCOMING

ye believed?' (Acts 19:2); and does not this clearly prove that one can be a Christian and yet need to receive the Holy Ghost afterward?"

To this we say both yes and no. There *is* a fullness of the Holy Ghost such as does not come to most Christians at conversion, and therefore is, in point of time, usually a second experience. But this is not the gift of the Holy Ghost, not the receiving of the Holy Ghost, not the baptism of the Holy Ghost as God's Word teaches. The Holy Ghost is received once and forever at conversion. He is a person. He comes in them once and forever, and to stay. We receive Him *then*—though we may not yield to him—for service, as well as for regeneration. The greater experience of His presence and power that follows conversion, sooner or later, is not the gift of the Holy Ghost, the receiving of the Holy Ghost, or the baptism of the Holy Ghost, as God uses those terms, but a fullness, in response to consecration, of that Holy Ghost who has *already* been given at regeneration. At Pentecost the Holy Ghost came down to form the Church, the mystic Body of Christ. On that great day Christ baptized the Church with the Holy Ghost. Wherefore, as each one of us by faith becomes a member of that Body, we are baptized with the same Spirit that dwells in that Body; we receive the gift of the Holy Ghost.

We cannot too clearly lay hold of this. For our deceitful natural heart is all too quick to take refuge in prayer, and waiting to receive, and thus dodge the real issue which is an absolute surrender to Him who has been received. So subtle is the flesh that it is glad, by waiting petition, to throw on God the burden of giving, if thereby it can evade the real issue which God has put upon us of yielding wholly to Him who has already been given. It is exactly matched by the case of the sinner who is far more willing to pray and wait on God for a blessing than to make the surrender that will bring the blessing.

But how about the Ephesian converts who were taught that they must receive the Holy Ghost *after* they had believed? Does not this prove that many, though Christians, have not received the Holy Ghost, and that this is the secret of their lack of power and victory? Now, if we will examine this instance in the light of God's own Word, with unbiased mind, we will see that this much-quoted passage (Acts 19:2) not only does not support the view that this was a receiving of the gift of the Holy Ghost by believers after regeneration, and thus proving our need of the same, but that it is one of the strongest proofs in God's Word that the apostles expected men to receive the Holy Ghost at conversion. In other words, the teaching of Paul corresponds exactly with that of Peter upon this great theme. We will recall from the preceding chapter that the simple conditions, as laid down by Peter, for receiving the gift of the Holy Spirit were repentance, and faith in the Lord Jesus Christ for the remission of sins. These two alone were necessary. But mark this, that both of these *were essential.* One was not sufficient. Men must repent *and* believe. For a man simply to repent of his sins, without faith in Jesus Christ for the remission of sins, would not bring the gift of the Holy Ghost, for one of the essential conditions would be missing. So also for a man to attempt to believe in the Lord Jesus Christ without repenting of his sins would not, and could not, bring the gift of the Holy Ghost, for the same reason—the absence, in this case of the necessary condition of repentance. We need not do anything more than God requires, but we dare not do anything less. Every Christian worker's experience confirms this. How often we meet with seekers after salvation who can find no witnessing peace of the Holy Ghost because there is some secret sin unsurrendered, some specific failure in repentance! Or again, some truly penitent one fails to find peace because he will not simply believe in Jesus Christ's atoning work for the remission of his sins. The evidence of multitudes of such cases confirms then this great truth of God's Word—that there are two conditions essential to receiving the gift of the Holy Ghost, namely, repentance and faith; and that the only reason anyone fails to receive Him is that he has not repented, or does not believe in Jesus Christ for the remission of his sins.

With this truth now in mind consider Acts 19: 1-6. Paul comes to Ephesus and, finding certain disciples, says to them, "Have ye received the Holy Ghost *since* ye believed" (Authorized Version), but "*Did ye* receive the Holy Ghost *when* ye believed" (Revised Version); thus showing that Paul expected them to receive Him at the time they turned from their sins. When they answer in the negative Paul begins at once to search for the cause, and he does so *exactly in line with the conditions laid down by Peter, as already quoted*. "Unto what then were ye baptized?" said Paul; and they said: "Unto John's baptism." "Oh, I see," says Paul in effect, "but don't you know that John baptized only unto *repentance?* Now, repentance is not enough to bring the gift of the Holy Ghost; you must also *believe* in Jesus Christ." And when they heard this, they believed on Jesus Christ and, baptized into *His* name, *received the Holy Ghost*. They were not believers at all as we are believers. They were practically believers under the Old Covenant, not under the New. They can be classed only with John's converts, who did not, and could not, receive the gift of the Spirit, inasmuch as they fulfilled only one condition, that of repentance. So far from being believers as we are, and being cited to prove that believers must receive the Holy Ghost as a second experience after conversion, these men, we are distinctly told, had not believed in Jesus Christ at all up to this time. Paul simply supplied the missing condition of salvation under the New Testament—faith in Christ, which should have been taught them when they repented. They stood

THE SECRET OF HIS INCOMING

in the place a penitent stands today who has honestly repented of his sins, but has not been instructed to believe in Jesus Christ for the remission of his sins. This failed to bring the gift of the Holy Ghost just as it would fail now. Then, too, the scriptural context, telling us exactly how this happened, seems to us forever to settle this mooted passage. If we go back to the preceding chapter we find an explanation that makes the whole episode as clear as sunlight. In verse twenty-four we are told: "A certain Jew named Apollos, . . . came to Ephesus, . . . being fervent in the Spirit, he spake and taught diligently the things of the Lord, *knowing only the baptism of John,*" that is, only the baptism of *Repentance* (19:4). While he was mighty in the Old Testament Scriptures, yet he evidently did not know God's full plan of salvation, and thus Aquila and Priscilla, when they heard him, "took him unto themselves and expounded unto him the way of God more perfectly" (v. 26), doubtless teaching faith in Christ for remission of sins. Apollos now goes to Corinth, and Paul, coming to Ephesus, finds Apollos' misinstructed disciples, a dozen men who had not received the Holy Ghost. Why? Simply because they had not believed in Jesus Christ. True, they were believers in the sense that John's disciples were believers, having "repentance toward God," but they had not "faith toward our Lord Jesus Christ." Paul therefore simply supplies the missing condition of New Testament conversion, and they receive the

Holy Ghost, not as a second experience of full-fledged believers, but as the first experience of those who had not believed in Christ at all. Instead of proving that the Christian man does not receive the gift of the Holy Ghost at conversion, but as a second enduement, this passage is one of the strongest proofs in the Word of God that the apostles expected men to receive the Holy Ghost at conversion, and, if not received, they simply proceeded to show that some one of the two simple conditions of New Covenant salvation had been neglected at the time of professed discipleship.

Again, take the case of the Samaritans recorded in Acts 8:5-25. "Here," it is said, "we are distinctly told that they believed Philip as he preached Christ, and that they were baptized" (v. 12). Why then was the Holy Spirit not received? It is suggested that there may not have been an honest repentance. For to Simon the sorcerer, who had professed belief and been baptized, Peter declared, "*Thy heart* is not right with God." Another, and likely more reasonable explanation is that God desired to show His condemnation of the enmity between Jew and Samaritan by using not Philip but two Jewish apostles, Peter and John, as the human instruments through which the outpoured Spirit came to the Samaritans.

A careful examination of these two chief passages cited to prove that the gift of the Holy Spirit comes as an after experience in the believer's life, will show, we believe, that they have no application to us as believers, but only prove that seekers after Christ must both repent and believe, in order to receive the gift of the Holy Ghost.

It follows too from this that every child of God has also been baptized with the Holy Ghost. The receiving of the Holy Ghost, and the baptism with the Holy Ghost we conceive to be absolutely synonymous, as God uses these terms. John baptized with water telling his disciples to believe on Him that should come after, and that then He would baptize them with the Holy Ghost. This was to be the distinguishing characteristic that was to mark baptism by the resurrected Christ. When men turned to God under the preaching of John he baptized them with water. But when they turn to Him in this Gospel age Jesus Christ baptizes them with the Holy Ghost. There is not a single instance that we recall where "baptism" with the Holy Ghost is made a subsequent experience of the believer. The apostles were again and again "filled," with fresh anointing, as it were, of the Spirit, but they were never baptized again. Nor are any converts who have received the Spirit in regeneration ever said thereafter to be baptized with Him. The reason is clear. Baptism was plainly an initial rite. It was administered upon entrance into the kingdom of God. Both baptisms stand, in relation of time, at the same place, whether John's with water, or Christ's with the Holy Ghost, namely, at the threshold of the Christian life, not at any subsequent milestone. Wherefore, when the baptism of the Spirit is urged now upon believers we may all agree with the thought behind it, namely, that of a fullness of the Spirit not yet known or possessed, for such a fullness is our birthright. Yet the expression itself is not a happy one in that it is never, to our knowledge, so used in the Scriptures, and therefore misleads men in attaching to a certain phrase a different meaning than God gives to it. Two speakers using a word to which each attached a different meaning would soon land in hopeless confusion. So has it been with this great theme, and it would clear up marvelously if we would not only study God's truth upon it, but adopt His phrases in describing it using "the gift," "the receiving," "the baptism" of the Holy Ghost exactly as He himself does in His own inspired Word.

In fact, the *receiving* of the Holy Ghost depends upon one set of conditions, and the *fullness* of the Holy Ghost upon another. Because we have not His *fullness*, we leap to the conclusion that we have not received *Him*. The truth is that we should accept forever the fact that we have received Him, and press on to know the secret of His fullness. Beloved, let your heart go out no longer in petition to receive the gift of the Holy Ghost, but let it be filled with praise that you have received Him, and that He is

THE SECRET OF HIS INCOMING

dwelling in you. Read again and again God's positive statements concerning it. Weigh them carefully. Recall your own experience of joy and peace when the Holy Spirit entered. Notice the constant statement in the Epistles that the believer is the sanctuary, the "holy place" where the Spirit indwells. Then remember that he who stands with God stands on sure ground. Let no one shake your confidence at this point. If any would, then repeat again and again His word, "Ye *are* the temple of the Holy Ghost, which *is* in you, which ye *have* of God," until you are forever settled in this glorious truth.

Then, though you have received Him, you are still painfully conscious of powerlessness, joylessness, fruitlessness in your life, know that there is a fullness of the Spirit who is in you; a life of abounding peace, and power, and joy, and love; a life of liberty; a life of victory over self and sin; that this life is for every child of God who will learn, and then fulfill, its conditions; that, therefore, it is for *you*. Then, knowing the secret of His incoming, the glorious fact that He is now in you, patiently waiting for you to act, press on to know the secret of His fullness.

To recapitulate, we believe God's Word teaches:

That every believer has received the Holy Ghost, the gift of the Holy Ghost, the baptism of the Holy Ghost.

That the simple secret of His thus incoming is—Repentance and Faith.

That there is a fullness of the Holy Ghost, greater than that usually thus received at conversion.

That there are certain conditions of this fullness, different from the conditions on which the Holy Ghost is received (that is, one may receive the Holy Ghost, yet not know His fullness); lastly:

That the secret of His fullness is—
what?

II

THE SECRET OF HIS FULLNESS

Yielding to Christ

Yield yourselves unto God.

Rom. 6:13.

Present your bodies . . . unto God.

Rom. 12:1.

Paul, a bond-slave of Jesus Christ.

Rom. 1:1, R. V.

The Secret of His Fullness

GRANTED, THEN, that we have received the gift of the Holy Ghost; that we have been baptized with Him; that He has come into our lives to abide forever. What then is the secret of His *fullness,* of His abundant life of peace, power, and love? We answer: *the absolute, unqualified surrender of our life to God, to do His will instead of our own.* Thus, when we surrender our *sins* and believe, *we receive* the Holy Spirit; when we surrender our *lives* and believe, we are *filled* with the Holy Spirit. *Receiving* the Spirit is God's answer to repentance and faith; the *fullness* of the Spirit is God's answer to *surrender* and *faith.* At *conversion* the Spirit enters; at *surrender* the Spirit, *already entered,* takes *full possession.* The supreme, human condition of the fullness of the Spirit is a life *wholly surrendered to God* to do His will. This is true:

1. *In Reason.* To our mind, all the clouds that have been hindering the clear outshining of this great truth into our soul will vanish away before him who will ponder carefully the great scriptural and experimental truth of *the twofold nature of the believer.*

Note first the situation of the sinner. He has but one nature—"the old man." He is declared absolutely to be *dead* in trespasses and sins. He has the self-life, but not the God-life within him. He walks in the flesh, and in that only. The Spirit may and does strive *with* him, but not *in* him, for only "he who is Christ's" hath that Spirit. But now comes a wonderful change. He repents and believes on the Lord Jesus Christ. What happens? He is born *again*, born *from above*, born of *God*, born of the *Spirit*. And what do these phrases signify? Simply that a new life, a divine life, the life of God, has come into him. God Himself, in the person of the Holy Spirit, has come to dwell in him; he has received the Holy Spirit. He has now what the sinner does not have— *a new nature*. But when the new life, the Spirit came in, did the old life, the "old man," go out? Alas, not he! If he had, then, *to receive* the Spirit would be at once and forever *to be filled with him*, for *He* would have *full* possession. But this is not the case. The old life does not go out when the new comes in; upon this God's Word and our own experience are painfully clear. But now, as a believer, he has, as it were, a dual nature. In him are both "the flesh" and "the Spirit"—the old life and the new. These two co-exist. Both *dwell* in him. But as deadly foes, they struggle for the mastership of his life. "The flesh lusteth against the Spirit, and the Spirit against the flesh." For each wants not

THE SECRET OF HIS FULLNESS

only to be *in* him but *to have full possession*. Each desires to *fill* him.

The problem is changed. It is no longer how shall he receive the Spirit. That is settled; he *has* received Him. But he finds him a *joint-tenant* with the flesh. Wherefore the question now is: Having two natures within him, how shall he be filled with one of them? How shall he know the fullness and abundant life of the Spirit, and be delivered from the life and power of the flesh?

The answer is clear. How else could he be filled save by *yielding himself wholly* to that one which he would have fill him? He has the power of choice; he can yield himself to either. Is it not clear that whatever life he yields himself to, that will fill him? When he once yielded himself a servant to the flesh (Rom. 6:19) was he not "filled with all unrighteousness"? (Rom. 1:29). Even so now, just in proportion as he yields himself to the Spirit (Rom. 6:19) will he not be filled with that Spirit? It is as though the sweet fresh air of spring should enter a ten-roomed house full of foul odors. You open up one chamber to it, but leave the rest closed and in possession of the old, fetid atmosphere. Truly the pure air has entered, but how can it fill the house until you yield that house wholly to it, throwing open every nook and cranny to its fragrant breath? Or, it is as though a fountain were fed by two strong springs bubbling up from the ground, one of water, the other of oil. There is no doubt that the fountain has received water, for it is constantly inflowing. Yet how can it be filled with water save as it yields itself wholly to its life-giving stream, and refuses to yield itself to the oil? Even so is it with the Holy Spirit. True He has come into every believer's heart, and abides there, and will abide forever. Yet every believer thus co-indwelt by the flesh and the Spirit may so continue to yield to the flesh as to thwart, choke up, and clog all manifestation of the fullness of the Spirit who is within him. This fact that, even after the Spirit has been received, there may be a mastership of Self in our lives through failure to yield to the Spirit, is a full and sufficient explanation of all lack of fullness of the Spirit. He who knows the awful power of that self-life in himself; its enmity with God; its carnality; its grieving and quenching of the Spirit; its deadly blighting of all the blessed fruits of the Spirit; its fierce and desperate resistings of his efforts to enter into the full life of the Spirit, needs no other explanation of the failure of fullness of the Spirit than *the fullness of Self*. The trouble is not the Spirit un-entered, but the Spirit un-yielded to, and thus shorn of opportunity to manifest the very fullness He desires. The remedy is clear, logical, inescapable: a refusal to yield the life longer to the mastership of self, and a surrender to the Spirit, that "the law of the Spirit of life in Christ Jesus may make us free from the law of sin and death."

THE SECRET OF HIS FULLNESS

It is true again:

2. *In Revelation.* God's Word is clear upon it. Paul again and again calls himself the "bond slave" of Christ, yielded to Him wholly, to do His will, not his own. "I beseech you therefore, brethren, by the mercies of God, that ye present your bodies a living sacrifice . . . unto God." "Yield yourselves unto God . . . neither yield unto sin . . . to whom ye yield yourselves to obey, his servants ye are . . . as ye have yielded . . . servants . . . to iniquity . . . now yield . . . to righteousness unto holiness" (Rom. 6:13, 16, 19). "But now being made free from sin, and become servants to God, ye have your fruit unto holiness" (v. 22); i. e., you know the power, blessing, fullness and fruitage of the Holy Spirit to whom you have now yielded. Notice both the impressive repetition and the significant position (Rom. 6) of his exhortation to yield ourselves to God. It follows the fifth chapter of Romans. That is, as soon as the believer, justified by faith, has received the Holy Ghost (v. 5), he is urged to yield himself to God, wholly and absolutely. Why? Because Paul knows the twofold nature of the believer; knows that with whatsoever he would be filled, to that he must yield; knows that if he would be filled with the Spirit he must yield to Him, otherwise he will go on living in the power and fullness of the flesh. *Thus the absolute yielding of our lives to God*

is the first great step after conversion urged in His Word.

Upon every convert, having received the Spirit, and while his heart is glowing with the love of Christ who has saved him, should be pressed home, earnestly and tenderly, the claim of that Christ upon his redeemed life, and His loving call to him to yield it to Him in absolute, unreserved surrender. There is no other way in reason, in revelation, or in practice. Alas for our blindness! Converts are exhorted to study the Word, to be diligent in prayer, to abound in good works, to give of their substance to the Lord, to be faithful in church services, to join her various societies, and to busy themselves in her countless round of activities. But (Woe unto us!) in omitting the one supreme condition which God reveals, we fail to lift the single flood gate which alone will let into our lives His coveted fullness. That this act of surrender is the pivot upon which the gate of His fullness swings open, is also seen in

3. *The experience of God's children.* Is it not true of all of you, beloved, who walk the pathway of the blessed life? The Holy Spirit painted in your secret soul pictures of a walk with God which persistently refused to fade, even amid all your failures and falling short of them. There were yearnings after a richness and fullness of life in Christ which never ceased to haunt your soul. There were voices that called you for years to untrodden heights of

THE SECRET OF HIS FULLNESS

communion, privilege, and service. You made many mistakes; you were misled by false teaching; you groped earnestly in the darkness after the truth. But now, with the peace and joy of an established life in Christ Jesus filling your soul, as you look back over the past do you not see that the pivotal point of blessing and fullness was the surrender of your life to the Lord Jesus Christ? Whether long years in coming to this crisis, or reaching it at a single bound, every consecrated child of God knows that this act of surrender to God was the supreme step that brought him into the fullness of the closer walk with God. Your experience may have been complicated, confused, difficult to interpret; but that this act of surrender was the culmination of it all, and this fullness of the Spirit, the outcome of such act, God's response of grace to that act, all will testify. The lives of such men as Carey, Martyn, Paton, and Livingstone, vividly show forth this truth. The fullness and power that marked their lives from the divine side went hand in hand on the human side with an unqualified, unwavering surrender of life in its fullest sweep, to do the will of Him that sent them. Only such can bring His fullness.

Again, that surrender is the secret of fullness is proven by—

4. *The Resistance of the Flesh.* We may be assured that a step which the self-life supremely op-

poses is the supreme step the Spirit would have us take. That point at which the Flesh masses its most desperate resistance must be the point to which the Spirit is most desirous of bringing us, the key-point of the situation. Above all else is the deliberate resolve to surrender the life to God this step, this point. How clamorously the hostile Self-life protests against it! We will lead meetings; sign pledges; fill official position; draw checks even to the half of our fortune; yea, do anything else; but how vehemently and desperately the Self-life opposes our yielding our life to God in full surrender! Does anyone question that self-will is the stronghold of the Flesh, and that the act of surrender storms the stronghold and is the act which the Spirit most desires and the Flesh most resists? Then let that man or woman try to make such a surrender. Let them say to God, "Here, Lord, I give up all my plans and purposes, all my desires and hopes, and accept Thy will for my life. Whatever Thou dost want, take; whatever Thou wouldst have come, send; wherever Thou wouldst have me go, lead; whatever Thou wouldst have me surrender, reveal. 'Lo, I come to *Thy* will.'" Immediately how the powers of the Flesh will assail this decision! What clamorous protests! What fierce hostility! What agonizing struggles! What deathly swoonings of the soul at the mere thought! What bitter tests of pride and reputation! What sweeping sacrifices loom up unthought of before! The pulpit, the mission field, yielded idols surrendered professions, or occupations or possessions; how these all start up like specters before the trembling soul! That day on which a child of God decides to yield his will to God will scarce have passed its meridian ere he will stand appalled at the revelation of his own unwillingness to do God's will; will be astonished and humiliated beyond measure at the desperate and repeated onslaughts of the Self-life, to drive him from the new stand he has taken. Just as the frantic cries and wild flutterings of the mother bird prove that your disturbing hand is near her nestlings, so does the passionate resistance of Self to the consecration of your life prove that through that act the Self-life is in deadly peril of overthrow under the mighty hand of God. Child of God, does not this very shrinking, this fierce enmity of the flesh, prove that his stronghold is unmasked, that his secret is betrayed, that the very thing which he most vehemently resists is that, above all others, which God wants you to do? Have you done it? For:

5. *There is no substitute for your act of surrender.* When God states a condition of blessing, no other condition, however good elsewhere, can be substituted. This is why all your crying, and waiting, and petitioning—yea, even agonizing before God—have accomplished naught but to leave you grieved, disappointed, and dazed at lack of answer. You have been praying instead of obeying. Prayer is all right *with* obedience, but not *instead* of it. "Obedience

is better than sacrifice." So is it better than prayer *if* it is the thing God is asking. We are not petitioning God; He is petitioning us! Hear Him through His servant Paul: "I beseech you, brethren, by the mercies of God, that ye present your bodies a living sacrifice." Have you done this? When we petition God to do something for us, we expect Him to act. When God petitions us to make Him a present of our bodies as a living sacrifice He expects us to act. But lo, we turn and begin to pray, for, we say, is not prayer a good thing? Indeed, it is, but not well spent if used to dodge obedience! How subtle the flesh is! How in our blindness we do play at cross-purposes with God! "Abraham," said God, "because thou hast done this thing, I will bless thee" (Gen. 22:16). And what was this thing upon the doing of which the blessing of God came to him as never before? It was the yielding of his all to God in the surrender of his son. Child of God, have you done this thing? No other thing will avail. Constant prayer, importunate entreaty, wearisome waiting, attempts at believing, reckoning it done—all these are of no avail if you will not do this thing. This unyielded life is the very citadel of Self. God will not force it. But when its key, the Will, is voluntarily handed over to Him, then He floods the life with His fullness of blessing. Would you know His "I will bless thee"? Then "do this thing." Absolutely, unreservedly, confidingly yield yourself, your life, your all into His hands for time and eternity.

THE SECRET OF HIS FULLNESS

It will not do, in lieu of this, to give money, to give time, to give service, only. Thousands are trying thus to silence conscience and rob God. We must needs give *ourselves*. How grieved would that true lover be whose betrothed would answer his petition for her heart, herself, by proffering her purse, houses, or lands! How much more must God be grieved by our poor attempts to bribe Him by giving Him everything else except the one thing He wants—*ourselves*. "My son, give me thine heart." There is a giving which is *instead of* ourselves; and there is a gift *of* ourselves. One is the poor bribe of legalism to Love; the other the joyful response of love to Love. So in falling short of giving ourselves to God, we fall short of the one supreme gift He desires. For God gave Himself, gave all to us. If our response to the Lover of our soul falls short of the truehearted surrender of ourselves, we thereby show that we do not fully trust Him. But the shadow of such distrust haunting the unsurrendered heart is the barrier that keeps it from the fullness of God. For God cannot give fullness of the Spirit to him who does not have such fullness of trust as to yield his life to Him. Wherefore, beloved, knowing that naught but this can bring to your heart His fullness of life, see to it that you omit it not. Know too, that

6. *The responsibility for this fullness of the spirit is, in a tremendous sense, in your own hands.* The question now rests with you. Not that it is not all of

God and of grace. It is. But in Christ Jesus the grace phase of it is complete. That is, God has already done all He can do for us in giving Christ. He "hath blessed us with every spiritual blessing in the heavenlies in Christ Jesus." Do we want God to pour out the fullness of the Holy Spirit? He has done so in Christ. "In him dwelleth all the fullness of the Godhead bodily" (Col. 2:9). Do we want God then to put us "in Christ" where the fullness dwells? He *has* done so, for "of Him are ye in Christ Jesus" (I Cor. 1:30). There is but one thing left, and that is yours. It is to so yield yourself to the Christ to whom you are united as to give Him opportunity to pour forth His fullness in and through you. This you must do. Do not attempt to throw the responsibility on God. He stands pledged to give you to know His fullness so soon as *you* surrender your life wholly to Him, but He does not stand pledged to surrender it for you, or to make you surrender it. He will not coerce your will. There He stops and waits—as He has been waiting for you. Do not say, either, "I have prayed, I have waited, I have wrestled and agonized, I have tried to believe it done," and the like. Do you not see that in all this you are calling on God to do something instead of obeying His command to do something yourself? The question is, have you yielded? Bought with a price, and not your own, have you taken your hands off your own life and consecrated it wholly, unflinchingly, eternally to the Lord Jesus Christ, to be His loving bond-slave forever? It is not now a question of His fullness; that is limitless. It is a question of your receptiveness, your surrender. Is He worthy of trust, of absolute trust? Then how far will you trust Him? How absolutely will you yield to Him? With what self-abandonment will you throw yourself upon Him? How far up toward the height of His perfect surrender will you climb? He will meet you where you meet Him. The only limit to His fullness is that which you impose in the limitation of your surrender. The more absolutely, sweepingly, irrevocably you yield yourself, time, talents, possessions, plans, hopes, aspirations, purposes—yea, all to Jesus Christ, vouching yourself His loving bond-slave to do and suffer His will, the more you shall know the blessed fullness of His Spirit. You may have all the fullness you will make room for. In a profound sense it rests with you. What a tremendous thought! To go through all the long years of life with the privilege, peace, and power of the blessed life within your grasp at any hour and yet to have missed it!

And are you faint-hearted, timorous, slow to trust Him absolutely? Are you loath to surrender your will, and afraid of His will? Think a moment what that will is for you. The bleeding Son of God hanging between Heaven and earth for you; translation from death to eternal life; sons and daughters of God; fullness of His spirit; peace, joy, fellowship in Him; instant, jubilant glorification at His coming;

triumphant sharing in His Kingship; eternal ages of unending bliss in His presence—this is His known will for you. And yet you fear His will! The soul's high treason, this, against its awful, loving Lord! Beloved, at the very core of your spiritual life nestles a deadly cobra of unbelief which you would do well, by this one deliberate, trustful act of surrender, to crush, before it strikes its fangs deeper into your heart. The daring cliff-climber, trusting a frail rope, swings out with dauntless heart over the dizzy abyss, while beneath him the cruel rocks and roaring, treacherous sea, eagerly wait to slay him if he falls. But you, beloved, when you this day swing out in blind and simple trust in Him, will find no cruel fate awaiting you, but the strong hands that catch you were pierced—for you; the side to which you are pressed in loving embrace was riven—for you; the heart that throbs with joy at your obedience once broke—for you. Yet, the Christ who beseeches you is the Christ of love, desiring to fill you with His own fullness of love. Therefore fear Him not, but, entering into the secret place, fight the battle; endure the suffering of the cross; cease not until you have honestly laid your life at His feet; and "He will give thee the desire of thine heart."

Trust

THERE IS BUT ONE ATTITUDE that the life surrendered to Him dare take to know His fullness, and that is: to trust and obey. Upon the necessity of obedience we need hardly dwell here, but may simply say that it is the very essence of surrender, which is naught else but an absolute yielding of our wills to obey the will of another—even our Lord and Master. As the whole catastrophe of the fall is wrapped up in the doing of our own will, the whole blessedness of the new life is involved in "Lo, I come to do Thy will." In surrender is obedience; in obedience is surrender. That surrender which is a supreme act of obedience marks and means the beginning of a habit, a life of obedience to the Holy Spirit to whom we have yielded. So clearly is obedience inwrought in the very idea of surrender that we shall not dwell long upon it in our brief limits, but pass on to some thoughts upon its mated truth of Trust.

1. *Trust Him as indwelling*. There is, as we have seen, an erroneous teaching which essays to meet our spiritual powerlessness and barrenness by

asserting that we have not received the gift of the Holy Ghost, have not been baptized with the Holy Ghost, and that what we need is to wait for the promise of the Comforter, and then, when He comes in, all this will disappear. We have endeavored very simply to show that this is unscriptural, confusing, and misleading; that the believer does not surrender his life in order to have the Spirit enter but because He has entered; that the believer's life does not climax in the incoming of the Spirit but starts with it; that such indwelling is not the capstone but the base-stone of the entire structure of his inner life and outward service. Yet so accustomed have we become to the former view of this subject that the first thing we do after we yield our lives in surrender to Him is to begin to look for Him to enter, to wait for the promise, to expect His indwelling. Now it is as against all this that we urge the child of God to trust in His indwelling. Do not await it, do not expect it, accept it; do not seek for it, recognize it; do not build up to it, build upon it as a sure foundation. "What?" you say, "Accept the indwelling of the Spirit as a fact before surrender without any conscious incoming after it, without any feeling or emotional experience of His acceptance of my yielded life?" Precisely. Accept the fact of the Spirit's indwelling exactly as you accepted the fact of the remission of your sins when you believed on Jesus Christ, by evidence a thousandfold

THE SECRET OF HIS FULLNESS

more certain and reassuring than your shifting feelings, namely, the eternal, immutable Word of God.

That Word is plain. God asks of you only one thing, namely, that you examine yourself and see whether you are in the faith; that is, a believer (II Cor. 13:5). If so, then He assures you that He dwells in you; He reiterates again and again that your body is the temple of the Holy Spirit, who is in you, whom ye have of God, who dwells in you forever (I Cor, 3:16, etc.). He does not ask you to inspect your emotions for this, but to take His word for it. He does not ask you to wait for a feeling but to rest upon a fact, accepting His plain word as the evidence of that fact. Then, apart from any consciousness of His indwelling, as you believe in, accept, recognize, and act upon that indwelling, you soon find it to be a glorious fact. A good old colored saint, when asked how he had become so conscious of the Spirit's presence in his heart, replied: "Jess you believe He's there and He is there." And so trust in His indwelling. Do not deny or await it, but believe and accept it. Like Brother Lawrence, "practice the presence of God" and you shall soon experience it. "Act as though I were in you, and you shall know that I am in you." Right here it will much aid this trust in His indwelling if we will but grasp the important truth that is here in place, namely:

Distinguish between The Indwelling of the Holy Ghost and The Manifestation of the Holy Ghost, in His fullness. By indwelling is meant His presence in us; by manifestation the consciousness of that presence. Now the indwelling of the Holy Ghost depends upon our union with Christ, through faith, as we have seen. But the manifestation of the Holy Ghost depends upon our obedience to His commandments (John 14:21) (in this case the call to yield ourselves to Christ). Wherefore the Spirit's indwelling depends upon our standing, His manifestation upon our state. The first is a question of union, the second a question of communion (in this case through obedience). The first is accomplished by God, and is a permanent fact in the believer's life independent of his feeling about it or consciousness of it. Assuredly! "Of God are ye in Christ Jesus." (I Cor. 1:30). It is God who united you, child of God to Jesus Christ, and united you forever. At that union the Holy Ghost came into you, and came to dwell forever (John 14:16). That the Holy Ghost indwells in you forever is as much a fact as that Jesus took away your sins forever. If you are a child of God the Spirit dwells in you; if you are an obedient child the Spirit manifests Himself in you. Your birth does not depend upon yourself; you were born of God; but your walk does depend upon yourself, and with it the Spirit's manifestations. Indwelling should be associated with sonship; manifestation with **obedience** and com-

THE SECRET OF HIS FULLNESS

munion. Now sonship is the gift of God and irrevocable, and so is the indwelling of the Spirit. But obedience and communion being largely in our hands are variable, wherefore, so is manifestation. Thus one of the deadliest errors we fall into is to make manifestation the test of indwelling, instead of the test of obedience to, and communion with, Him who is already indwelling. Never doubt the indwelling of the Spirit because you do not feel His presence, any more than you doubt that Jesus died for you, because you do not feel that death. If we are saved only when we feel saved, and the Holy Spirit indwells only when we are conscious of His indwelling, then woe unto us, for the Spirit ceases to dwell in us, and we are lost men and women whenever we stumble or disobey in our walk with God! What a disastrous and appalling error to fall into! Whereas when we see that His indwelling depends upon an unchangeable fact—our eternal union with Christ by faith—but the consciousness of that indwelling upon a changeable state—namely, our walk with God—then any decline in that consciousness of His presence will never lead us to doubt His indwelling, but only stir us to scan our lives if so be that we may be following Him so far off in the path of communion and obedience as to have lost the shining of His manifested presence. We see from this also our need to:

2. *Trust Him as to manifestation.* Do not dic-

tate to Him the kind of feeling of fullness you desire. Do not insist upon a sudden flood-tide of emotion. Do not pitch upon some other man's experience, heard or read of, and expect God to duplicate it in you. Trust all this to Him. We are prone both at conversion and consecration to come to the Lord with a previously formed conception of the exact sort of an experience we are to have. And are we not almost invariably disappointed? Why? Because God knows far better than we just what feeling to give us. Does not our very surrender to do and receive His will, instead of our own, carry with it a loving submission to Him in this matter of manifestation, as in all others, accepting sweetly just such individual measure of fullness as *He* deems best? Paul had such wonderful manifestations of spiritual things as to need a thorn in the flesh "lest he should be exalted overmuch." There is a suggestion here that the Lord knows just what form and degree of fullness to give each one of us, to keep us from spiritual pride, or exaltation. Therefore, leave it all to Him. Whether sudden or gradual; quiet or jubilant; great peace or great power; it matters not. Let us be concerned to meet the conditions of promise, and God will always take care of the fulfillment of the promise. He who yields himself most fully to the cross of Christ in surrender, leaving the whole question of experience of fullness with God, will come sooner and more abundantly into its blessedness than he who, ignor-

THE SECRET OF HIS FULLNESS

ing the conditions of full discipleship, spends his time awaiting tongues of fire and sound of rushing, mighty wind.

Nothing is more hurtful than to be constantly inspecting our own inner lives to see if God is fulfilling His promise in our experience. It is like the child constantly digging up the seed to see if it has sprouted. The question of the experience of fullness of the Spirit belongs to the Lord. It is His gracious work alone. He has promised, "I will manifest myself; this is My part; leave this to Me." The supreme thing for us to do is to fulfill the conditions placed upon us through which God's blessing comes, and trustfully leave His part to Him. The less we are concerned and anxious about the manifestation of His fullness, the sooner will it come. Perfect faith in God, as we have seen, is all essential to knowing His fullness. But is there not in this scanning each pulse of feeling as it comes, a subtle unbelief, a fear that perhaps God will not be faithful even though we are? And back of it all are we not perhaps more anxious for the blessing, the joy, the feeling of the Spirit's fullness than eager, and willing, and quick to yield our lives to our blessed Lord, even though no feeling should follow it? Therefore, beloved, be occupied with an honest, complete, heart-searching surrender, and leave all else in God's hands.

3. *Trust the Spirit as He works IN you.* At no point is a simple, unwavering trust in Him needed more than just here. For consider first how utterly incapable you yourself are of shaping, fashioning, purifying the life you have just yielded into His hands. How full of errors and failures it has been! How far it falls short even of our own human, not to speak of His divine, ideal for it! How sinful, weak, and inconsistent! As you have striven, labored, and battled in your efforts to develop it, how colossal has seemed the task, how hopeless the outcome! You are wrestling not against flesh and blood, but against principalities and powers; against the rulers of darkness; against those who laugh in scorn at your self-efforts to overcome them. You know not the power of evil; you know not the might of the Self-life; you know not God's power to cope with both. Apart from God you know not what armor you need; what weapons to wield; what battles must be fought; what crisis the unknown future will bring; how the old man shall be "put off"; how the new shall be put on; where your lot shall be cast; or what field God has prepared for you. As you sit and ponder, how hopeless it is for you, a mortal man or woman, to try to mould and shape a life that is immortal in its service, scope, and destiny, sweeping far into the mystic depths of eternity in its outcome; do you not realize how foolish you have been even to attempt to possess and control that life instead of yielding it at once to the

THE SECRET OF HIS FULLNESS

Holy Spirit who brought it into being? Can you do anything else than trust Him wholly and absolutely with it, in view of your utter failure and inability to fashion it for the ministries, not only of this life, but of eternity?

But on the other hand, hark how simple and absolutely you can trust the Spirit to work in the life you have yielded. Did He not bring you into being? Does He not know you as only the all-seeing God can? Is He not acquainted with your sins and weaknesses; fleshliness and failures; powers and talents; regretted past, unsatisfied present, and unknown, eternal future? Does He not know just when you need chastening, and when rebuke? When to press hard with the Cross, and when to comfort with His own joy? When to use the knife and when to pour in the soothing ointment? Just how to mould and fashion; chisel and cut; straighten and strengthen; pound, hammer and polish until the statue is as He would have it—like the Son? *Trust* Him. When He leads you into paths that wound your faltering feet; confronts you with a future that lowers dark and threatening; hems you in with providences that seem harsh and mysterious—in all these stand still; whisper to yourself, "It is God that worketh," and— *Trust* Him. For the Spirit must needs work in you before He can work through you. He must purify the gold before He can send it forth as sterling coin, the choicest of His mintage. And if you will not stay under His hand, even when He works ever so strangely, how can He accomplish His deepening, enlarging, enriching purpose in your life? *Trust Him as He works in you.* It matters not that His dealings with you are strange, mysterious, even confusing; that this is not the way in which you would like Him to work; that He is not sending you experiences of the kind or degree you expected. You may not indeed understand all this, but *He* does, "for it is *God* that worketh *in* you."

4. *Finally trust Him to work THROUGH you.* It is one thing to work for God; it is another to have God work through us. We are often eager for the former; God is always desirous of doing the latter. One of the important facts in the surrender of the life is that it is the attitude which gives God the chance to work His perfect will through us. For it is God that is working to evangelize the world; it is God who has laid the plans for it; it is God who has the power to successfully execute them. Now the God who is the ruler of the universe does not want us to plan, and worry, and work for Him. For while He appreciates our purposes toward Him, yet they may be all athwart His purposes for, and through us. What He wants is not our plans, but our lives, that He may work *His* plans through us.

Now God will certainly do this through every life that is yielded to Him, if we simply trust Him so to do, and follow Him as He leads us on. His word

THE SECRET OF HIS FULLNESS

upon this is clear. "For we are . . . created in Christ Jesus unto good works which God hath before ordained that we should walk in them" (Eph. 2:10). God has an ordained plan of good works in Christ Jesus, and as each member of the body of Christ yields himself or herself to Him absolutely to do His ordained works, He will give to, and reveal to, that individual member his or her particular works, so that they may walk in them. This is a plain promise of guidance, not only into a practical lifework for each one yielded to him, but the lifework which God has ordained for each one of His children "from before the foundation of the world." Is this incredible to you, beloved? Nay, anything else is incredible! For that God should have a purpose for every drop of dew glittering in the morning sunlight; for every blade of grass that upsprings from the earth; for every flower that blooms on hill or heath; and yet not have a plan for the lives of the men and women for whom these were created, is indeed in the last degree incredible! And do you reply that there are myriads of lives of His children apparently afloat upon the stream of a purposeless existence? Alas, yes. But it is because God cannot reveal His will to an unrenounced Self-will; cannot make clear His plans to a life full of Self-plans. Such unyielded Self-plans and Self-will become the fleshly cataract that veils the spiritual vision to God's plan and God's will. But when you yield your life wholly to Him, God will take away that veil and sooner or later show you your lifework. This is true, it matters not how dark the way is now, how hedged in by adverse circumstances, how trying or complicated your present position. You may have to wait; you must needs be patient; but God will assuredly extricate you from all entanglements, and work out His blessed will through you, if you will but trust, wait, and obey as He guides. Many a life once so hemmed in as to seem beyond hope of freedom, is now witnessing for Christ in the distant dark lands.

We have a dear friend who, soon after being saved, was led to see the truth and glorious privilege of the surrendered life, and gave that life simply and trustfully to God. He was a busy man, shut in all day behind a counter, in a position that seemed to bar him absolutely from being led into any lifework God might have planned for him. Yet mark the result. Reading one day an interesting item in a religious journal, he was led to write the author and ask permission to print and circulate it free, in tract form. This was willingly granted, and the little leaflet began to go out on its errand of blessing from the hand-press of our friend, who was an amateur printer. As the months went by, other leaflets were added; voluntary offerings began to come in for the work; the few hundred tracts crept up into thousands, and hundreds of thousands; stories of conversion of sinners, and blessing to God's chil-

THE SECRET OF HIS FULLNESS 71

dren poured in from the logging camps of Michigan, the prisons of Wisconsin, the country at large, and the mission fields of distant lands. In the two or three years after this work began one million tracts have been sent out free; the Word of God has been circulated to an extent, and with results that eternity alone will reveal; and our busy friend is one of the happiest of the great King's servants, in the consciousness of being in a work which God has planned for him, and gave to him when he yielded his life to Him. Even so will God assuredly lead every surrendered child of His out from the place of darkness, inquiry, and uncertainty, into the light and joy of that God-planned, and God-empowered service which is to be his glad lifework if he will only *Trust* Him who works *in* us, and desires to work mightily *through* us.

Manifestation

BY INDWELLING IS MEANT, as we have seen, the presence of the Spirit in us as believers; by manifestation is meant the consciousness of His presence; the inner revelation of the Spirit to our spirit. Concerning this, notice:

1. *Its Certainty.* Will there be such manifestation of the fullness of the Spirit when we yield our lives to Him? Will we be aware of a great inner change in those lives? Will there be a conscious transformation, a conscious new estate of Christian experience? We answer: Is the sluggish, stagnant river conscious of the inrushing waters of the sea, as it feels the throb and rush of her cleansing tides? Is the dark, gloomy old castle conscious of the fresh, sweet air that fills its wind-swept chambers, as they are flung wide open? Are the sightless eyes, that have been veiled for years in hopeless darkness, conscious of the bright light of day, when it first breaks upon their enraptured vision? So, assuredly, is there a conscious manifestation to the soul that has given itself, for all time and all things, to God. There must be, there will be a change; a realization

THE SECRET OF HIS FULLNESS 73

of His presence to a degree never known before; a consciousness that the greatest crisis in the spiritual life has been passed. Nor does it matter whether such manifestation of His fullness bursts upon us like the sudden outflashing of the sun from behind dark clouds, or steals upon us like the slow-increasing glow of the morning twilight, gradual, but sure. Enough for us to know that such manifestation does come; that He does reveal Himself in fullness, power, and blessing never known before. His beseeching us to present our bodies to Him was not idle entreaty; our yielding to Him was not vain experiment. He fulfills His promise, "I will manifest myself, as I do not unto the world." Henceforth there is height and depth, peace and power, joy and blessing, communion and service, prayer and praise, such as the past has never possessed. To that soul who gives himself wholly to God, life is transformed beyond his fondest hopes; the blessings of the Abundant Life become richer and fuller as the days go by; God does exceedingly abundantly above all he can ask or think. He is "strengthened with might by His Spirit in the inner man"; "filled with all the fullness of God"; made to "abound more and more"; and out of this abundance overflow ministry, testimony, and blessing to those about him.

2. *Its Individuality—manifestation will vary with the individual.* Two men, absorbed in conversation, stand upon a railroad track, not noting the ap-

proach of a train swiftly bearing down upon them. Just in time both are snatched by friendly hands, from the awful death impending. To both, as they turn away with blanched faces, the same event has come, namely, rescue from a terrible death under the wheels of the rushing, roaring train. But mark how differently it affects them. One's eyes fill with tears, his voice trembles with suppressed emotion, and his heart is quietly uplifted in profound gratitude to God. The other, fairly ecstatic in his emotion, leaps for joy, embraces his rescuers, and exultantly recounts the story of his deliverance to all whom he meets. The same blessing has come to both, but the experience manifests itself diversely, because their individual temperament is different. Just so is it here. Two of God's children yield their lives to Him in entire surrender. In response to that surrender the same event will come to them both—a fullness of the Spirit never known, never thought possible before. But the manifestation, the experience of that fullness, will not be the same in both; it will necessarily vary with the individual temperament. For God not only gives the fullness, but He also made the vessels which contain that fullness, and has made them all slightly different. The cup, vase, and goblet of gold, are all full, but the water within them takes the shape from the fashioning form of the vessel. The light which streams through the electric wires is all the same, but it takes its tints from the many-colored globes through which

THE SECRET OF HIS FULLNESS

it glows. Paul and John were both men mightily filled with the Holy Ghost; yet how strikingly His manifestation was modified by their individual temperaments. Paul is exultant, fiery, and vehement. He breaks forth, time and again, into shouts of triumph, praise, and joy. His wondrous life burned and flamed with love for Christ, with an intensity that seemed about to consume it at any moment. Life seemed all too short for his eager soul to compress into its fleeting moments all the devotion, zeal, and enthusiasm of the highest-keyed, widest-ranged life the Holy Ghost has pictured in the early church. Paul was assuredly full of the Holy Ghost, and thousands of martyrs and missionary heroes, gifted with that same intensity of temperament, and inspired by the vision of that Spirit-filled life, have set before them the Pauline type of Christian experience as their own desired ideal, and, yielded to God, have marvelously attained to, and exemplified it, in service and sacrifice for the same Master. And yet that man who thinks he is not filled with the Holy Spirit unless enjoying the same kind and degree of manifestation as Paul, may be far astray from the truth. For, on the other hand, turn to John. No man was closer to the heart of Jesus Christ than he. He leaned upon His bosom; he felt the throb of His Master's heart-life as none other; he interpreted the inmost secrets of His soul. His writings breathe out the very spirit of Christ and bring us into the very presence chamber of a holy God.

Quiet, contemplative, devotional, his soul does not seem to break forth into exultant shout like Paul's, but to be rapt, absorbed, lost in the vision of the Christ. Yet John, the beloved disciple, the confidant of Christ, was as surely full of the Holy Ghost as was Paul, the great apostle to the Gentiles. In the holy, quiet, close walk with God of John's life, we see pictured a type of manifestation of the Spirit which has reproduced itself in thousands of godly lives, whose constant communion, ministry of prayer, and quieter forms of service, are unspeakably precious in God's sight, and bear the assured mark of His fullness. The Johns, and Rutherfords, and Bengels of God's fold, are as surely filled with the Spirit as the Pauls, the Judsons, and the Patons. Let us therefore, when we have yielded our lives, be grateful to God for just such individual manifestation as He may, in His grace, vouchsafe us. In coveting some other man's type of experience, because it comports more with our idea of what the manifestation of the Spirit's fullness should be, let us beware lest we disparage, and dishonor what God has bestowed upon us. If He grants us wondrous visions, fills us with spiritual ecstasies, catches us up into the third heaven; it is well. But if He apportions to us a quieter experience; pours out upon us the spirit of supplication; fills us with a peace as profound as other men's joy is rapturous; anoints us with power in prayer, instead of power in the pulpit; this too is well. For He knows, and "the Spirit divideth asunder severally as He will."

3. *Its accompaniment:—Suffering.* In I Peter 4:1, 2, this truth is stated: "Forasmuch then as Christ hath suffered for us in the flesh, arm yourselves likewise with the same mind; for he that hath suffered in the flesh hath ceased from sin; that he no longer should live the rest of his time in the flesh to the lusts of men, but to the will of God." The flesh—the carnal nature—which in Christ was sinless is in us sinful; is the sphere in which sin works, "the body of sin," as it were. Therefore, in yielding our lives wholly to God to do His will, the old self-will, the flesh-life, must feel the touch of the Cross of Christ, for it is only as it is put in the place of crucifixion with Christ, through surrender and faith, that we can cease to do our own will, and come to do the perfect will of God. This means suffering, and the Word tells us plainly that we are to "arm ourselves likewise with the same mind," and expect to suffer in the flesh, in order to "no longer live the rest of our time in the flesh to the lusts of men, but to the will of God." Now, in seeking to know the fullness of the Spirit, we meet just such an experience. When yielding our lives to God, instead of the great manifestation of peace and joy of the Spirit we anticipated, we are troubled at finding one totally different. We come instead into a place of struggle, and of soul-agony; a consciousness of

fierce resistance, and of keenest suffering; of turmoil, uncertainty, and distress. Instead of light is darkness; instead of peace, a dire unrest; instead of fullness, a seemingly utter spiritual void, and barrenness in our souls; instead of advance, an apparently backward step. All the while continues this sense of intense, awful, inward suffering, which we can neither define, describe, nor understand, save that it is so utterly diverse from our expectation as to throw us into almost hopeless confusion. And yet this experience is absolutely normal, explainable, and to be expected in every yielded life. "We do err not knowing the Scriptures." If we had known them we would "arm ourselves with the same mind," we would expect, in advance, exactly this experience. Let any believer who comes into this crisis be not confounded, or discouraged thereby, for it is sure evidence that God is going to bring him into the place of fullness for which his heart yearns. The journey to the upper room of Pentecost must needs be by a place called Calvary; God has the self-same place for self as for sins—the Cross of Christ; The man who cried, "It is no longer I but Christ that liveth in me," first cried, "I have been crucified with Christ." But it hurts to be crucified with Christ! And so there is darkness, and struggle, and agony, and suffering. Nevertheless, "fear not, only believe," for "if we have been united with Him by the likeness of His death, we shall be also by the likeness of His resurrection," and out of it all will come God's own rest, peace and power.

4. *Its time—the time of surrender.* As has been stated, we are not, the instant we have yielded to God, to begin to scrutinize our inner experience to see if He has fulfilled His promise of manifestation. For the moment of professed surrender is not always the moment or real surrender to God, since there may be something in our lives concerning which there is conscious failure to yield, and which will thus hinder the Spirit's manifestation at the moment of apparent surrender. Yet, as we look back over our lives, we clearly see the general truth that the experience of the Spirit's fullness was God's response to our surrender, and we definitely link the two together in the time-records of our spiritual lives. This clears up the mooted point whether the manifestation of the fullness of Christ is, or is not, an after-conversion experience, a so-called "second blessing." If, as has been seen, the experience of the Spirit's fullness is linked in fact, and in time, with the surrender of our life to God, then the only question is, when did we so surrender? If, at conversion, we not only trusted Christ for salvation, but also yielded our lives to Him in entire surrender, then we not only received the Spirit, but came also to know His fullness. But, if an interval of greater or less length occurs between our salvation and our consecration to God, then of

necessity the fullness of the Spirit must be, as it usually is, an experience subsequent to conversion. Logically, such an interval is always necessary; practically, it may be so short as to make the two experiences almost simultaneous; usually there is such an interval, long, weary and needless, in which the soul gropes after the unknown, or resists the known truth. Logically, such an interval is needful because the appeal to consecration presumes salvation, and is grounded upon it. "I beseech you therefore, brethren, *by the mercies of God*, that ye present your bodies a living sacrifice . . ." (Rom. 12:1.) It is the love which springs up in our hearts because Christ has saved us, that prompts us to yield our lives to Him. The yielded life is the response of the redeemed to their Redeemer, and it is not until after they have experienced the love of "Him who first loved them," that their own hearts can be kindled with the love that prompts to surrender. Therefore, conversion must of necessity precede consecration.

Practically, the interval may be so short as to be almost unnoted. The same flood of grace that bears a soul into the kingdom of God, simultaneously fills his heart with such responsiveness of love as can find vent only in the instant surrender of the life. Happy are such! Paul seemed hardly saved until, in the attitude of consecration, he was crying out, "Lord what wilt thou have me to do?" Charles G. Finney, after he had found Christ as his Saviour,

THE SECRET OF HIS FULLNESS

testified that as he emerged from the depths of the woods, and walked toward his law-office, he found himself repeating aloud: "I must preach the Gospel." Almost unconsciously he had, in the very hour of his conversion, surrendered his life to God, and the vision of clients, briefs, and professional ambitions had fled away, before the vision of Him who died for him. The result was that the same night, while alone in his office, there came to him such a manifestation of the fullness of God as has been given to few men since the days of the early Church, the mere reading of which fills the heart with reverential awe at the vision of what God can do with the wholly yielded life.

Usually, there is a considerable interval between conversion and entire surrender to God. Yet, it is a needless, and unhappy one. It exists not because God desires or plans it, but because we are ignorant of this great heart-truth, or knowing, keep resisting Christ's call. Finally, after years of darkness or disobedience, we yield, and come into a haven of rest which we might just as well have entered years before, instead of long tossing on the troubled sea without.

5. *Its Progressiveness—manifestation of the Spirit's fullness may be progressive.* Not that the will to surrender is a process. It is a definite act, done once and for all, and it is well-pleasing to God as such. Yet few believers realize at the time the significance

and sweep of a complete surrender to God. For this reason the perfecting of this surrender is measurably a process, and there is a progressiveness of manifestation with it. In some lives this is less, in others, more marked. Some men and women give up their lives to God in an instant, with a sweep, absoluteness, and intensity of consecration that takes the breath of cautious, tardier souls, and God's seal of manifested fullness is as immediate, and impressive, in its response. Others yield slowly, and by degrees, to God, and their experience takes a like more gradual and progressive cast. We may illustrate somewhat like this: You own a valuable landed estate. Deciding, after due deliberation, to sell it, you did so in good faith, and are now about to transfer it. Strolling over it some day before the transfer, you discover, to your surprise, a fine, living stream of water of whose existence you had not known before, and which much enhances the value of your estate. It costs you considerable of a struggle to let this go with the land, for it was not in your knowledge when sold. But you are an honorable man, and finally yield, for the estate was sold "with all its appurtenances." Soon after this you discover out-croppings of coal upon the same farm, and wake up to the realization of the presence of a valuable coal mine. But it is now too late, and after a severe struggle you decide that the coal mine must go too, inasmuch as the sale was absolute and without reserve. As the day for the transfer comes, you one day discover traces of gold in the river bottom, and are soon astonished with the tidings that your vanishing estate is one of the richest gold-bearing tracts on the continent. And now comes a mighty struggle, a supreme test. You try to persuade yourself that gold mines were not included in the sale; that the price is wretchedly inadequate; that you are not in honor bound to complete the transfer. But in your heart you know that the sale was without reserve; that it included everything, even to the air above and the earth beneath that farm; and your God-given conscience pleads without ceasing until, at last, after a terrific struggle, you yield, and set your hand and seal to the deed which sweeps away so much more than you had ever foreseen. Even so it is in many lives. We yield ourselves absolutely and without reserve to God, and this, acceptable to Him, brings manifest blessings into our souls. But we do not begin to know the full scope and significance of such consecration to Christ, and, if we did, would perhaps shrink back appalled from a full-orbed vision of its meaning at the outset. Our blessed Lord knows this, and how compassionately and tenderly He meets it! Well pleased with our yielded wills He soon reveals some cherished idol, and shows it to be involved in our surrender in blank, as it were, to Him. Perhaps we struggle and resist, but our act of surrender was honest and sincere, so we yield it. Step by step He now leads on, showing us, as rapidly as we are able to bear it, how this act of surrender includes everything we hold dear. Finally, with added faith in His love from these experiences, He brings us face to face with our gold-mine, our Isaac, some treasure of self-will, affection, or pride, than which we would rather yield up all else in life, yea, our very life itself. But the deed has been drawn; there is no reserve; all must go. And so, out of the struggle, comes that perfecting of surrender which brings into our hearts His coveted fullness of manifestation. It should rejoice us much that there are intrepid souls whose challenge of, "Lord what wilt thou have me to do," He answers by a revelation of the sweep and scope of surrender, whose instant, fearless acceptance brings instant manifestation of His fullness. Yet how beautiful that He should thus lovingly and patiently, lead the more timorous and shrinking souls up the golden staircase of the yielded life, until, step by step, they too have attained to that glad height, which others conquer at a bound!

MY CONSECRATION

I believe Jesus Christ is dwelling in me by His Spirit because God's Word says so (II Cor. 13:5; I Cor. 6:19).

I believe He is seeking to work out His purpose through me (Eph. 2:10; John 15:16).

I realize that my life must be yielded to Him in order that He may accomplish this purpose (Rom. 6:13).

I hear His call to me, "I beseech you . . . present your body a living sacrifice . . . to God (Rom. 12:1).

I now heed His call.

This day I definitely consecrate my life to the Lord Jesus, to trust, obey and serve Him as best I know while life shall last. And I pray that He may enable me henceforth to live such a life of faith, love, and devotion to Him as I will wish to have lived when I see Him face to face.

Date............ Signed......................

This is not a pledge. It is a free-will offering. Do you know the supreme free-will offering you can bring to Jesus Christ in response to His unspeakable sacrifice for you? It is *Yourself*. The greatest tragedy of time and eternity is a *Lost Soul*. The next greatest is a *Lost Life*. I mean that of a Christian whose soul is saved but whose life is being lived for the world and for self instead of for Christ. For every man in Christ Jesus, God has a purpose, a plan, and a place. You will find them all when you consecrate your life to Him. And O, what you will miss both for time and eternity by living that life for the world.

Do not sign this card unless you mean it. Get alone with God in the quiet place. Think it over and pray it through. And then decide deliberately whether you, a redeemed child of God, can afford to live this one fleeting life of yours down here out of the will and purpose of God for it. That is supremely what consecration means. It is presenting your body a living sacrifice to Jesus Christ to live His glorious will for it, instead of your own selfish and self-centered one. What will you say to Him about Romans 12:1 when you meet Him in the glory?

III

THE SECRET OF HIS CONSTANT MANIFESTATION

Abiding In Christ

Abiding In Christ

WE COME NOW to the last phase of the threefold secret of the Holy Spirit. Its importance will be recognized in the following type of experience, not uncommon among believers. A child of God, brought by the Spirit under conviction as to this truth, sees God's claim upon his life, and lays it at His feet, a living sacrifice. In answer to that surrender there comes to him from God a fullness of power, blessing, and spiritual life, beyond his fondest imaginings, and his spirit rejoices in the riches of his fuller experience. So manifest is the Spirit's presence in his heart, so consciously is he filled with His life, that he feels as though he had reached a new state of spiritual power and experience which will never leave nor diminish. But, by and by, there comes a change. The brightness of the experience seems to dim; its power begins to wane; its manifestation to diminish. He still continues to "claim" what he feels is gone; to profess what he does not possess, in the hope that this may bring back the "blessing." But at last he breaks down in despair, and henceforth refers to all this as a "lost experience," a blessing which he once enjoyed, but which has now fled away. In such a case—only too common—what has happened? It is not that the Spirit has ceased to reside in such a believer; but He has ceased to reveal Himself in his former fullness. It is not a question of lost indwelling, but lost manifestation. The Blesser has not left, but the blessing has. The manifestation of the Spirit's fullness was perfectly satisfactory to him in kind, and degree, but not in performance. It failed in continuousness, slowly fading away like the flush of the twilight in a sunset sky. And why? What is the explanation of this default in continuance of manifestation?

1. In John 14:21 Christ states the general conditions of the manifestations of the Spirit, when He says: "He that hath my commandments and keepeth them . . . will manifest myself to him." Plainly referring here to the manifestation of Himself through the Spirit, He declares, as a great, universal truth, that the conditions of that manifestation are the keeping of His commandments, meaning by these, as we shall hereafter see, not the commandments of the Law, but those of Grace—Faith and Love—which fulfill the Law. In other words, Christ simply asserts that the manifestation of God comes to him who does the will of God. Thus, when the individual in the case cited was a sinner, the will of God for him as an unsaved man was to repent, and believe in the Lord Jesus Christ, unto the salvation of his soul. This he did, and at once there came the

THE SECRET OF HIS CONSTANT MANIFESTATION 91

manifestation of God at conversion; the Spirit, as we have seen, was received, and entered to dwell forever. And now, as time passes on, he sees that there is within him a Self-life which is enmity with the God-life, and that God's will for him is the giving up of all self-will, and the yielding of himself wholly to God to do His will. This, too, he does, and straightway there comes, at consecration, a mighty manifestation of God, in the fullness of that Spirit who was already received. To both these acts of doing God's will, God responded by manifesting Himself to the believer, just as He had promised. But now, instead of halting here, and claiming "the blessing," and trying to live the rest of his life on his experience, the believer should have pressed on to this kindred truth, that since the manifestation of the Spirit comes for him who does God's will, the continual manifestation of the Spirit can come only to him who continually does God's will. That is, though these times of manifestation have come from these acts of doing God's will, constancy of manifestation can come only from a continual doing, a daily living in the will of God. Thus, the surrender of the life is only the beginning of a life of surrender. The act of consecration must be incarnated into a life of consecration, if begun blessing is to be continued blessing. For consecration is rather the threshold, than the climax of the Spirit's fullness. It is not so much a star, which, once fixed, will forever illumine our lives with its radiance, without any further care from us, as it is a gateway, which needs to be constantly kept open, if the light which came in at its unbarring is to continue. And it is just here that the believer who is mourning over a "lost experience," has failed. He has learned the first and second secret of the Holy Spirit, but not the third and final one. He has *received* the Holy Spirit, through *union* with Christ; has been *filled* with the Holy Spirit, through *surrender* to Christ; but does not yet know the *constant manifestation* of that Spirit, through *abiding* in Christ. He has placed the climax of his Christian experience at Consecration, instead of at Abiding. He has received "the fullness"; claimed the "second blessing"; been made "perfect"; and then has done what no mortal man or woman dare do—has halted, and rested upon a so-called attained experience. Desiring solely to retain "the blessing" that has come to him, he stops short of the final and supreme secret of its intention—the secret of *abiding in Christ*. He is misled, confused, and disappointed, because he has failed to see that a man may have received the Spirit, been filled with the Spirit, and yet need to learn how to walk in the Spirit.

2. *The need of Abiding* arises from the two-fold nature of the believers—a truth already considered in another connection. If, when the new life of the Spirit filled the believer at surrender of the old life of the flesh vanished away, then there would be no need for the believer to learn the secret of Abiding.

THE SECRET OF HIS CONSTANT MANIFESTATION

But this is not the case. True, "our old man has been crucified." But he is crucified in Christ, and it is only as we abide in Christ that we realize this crucifixion and this resurrection life. The flesh still abides in the believer. Otherwise, why is he constantly exhorted to walk in the Spirit and not to walk in the flesh? He should not walk in it, and need not walk in it, but the fact that he may walk in it, and often does walk in it, proves that it is there. And being there, it must be evident that every time he yields to the flesh, and walks in the flesh, he that far frustrates, and checks the manifestation of the Spirit. Of very necessity this is true, for God cannot manifest Himself through the flesh. The mind of that flesh is "death"; is "enmity with God"; is the bitterest foe of the Spirit. Therefore, just so far as the believer walks in the flesh, yea in every act which he does in the flesh, the manifestation of the Spirit must so far cease. For the Spirit to do anything else would be for God to set His divine approval upon acts done by that which He hates, and has condemned to death—the flesh. It would be not only to let the flesh "glory in His presence," but it would be giving the very glory of His own holy presence to the flesh. It would be like bringing the Shekinah glory into the polluted temple of a heathen deity; like glorifying Dagon with the halo of divinity, instead of smiting him with the blow of divine judgment. Even though a man has been filled with the Spirit at surrender, yet God cannot set His seal to a life of non-conformity to His will, by continuing through it a manifestation of the Spirit due to a past act of obedience. The believer needs clearly to see this. He needs to understand that since manifestation comes to him who does the will of God, therefore every time he does the will of the flesh instead that manifestation must be clouded. There is conscious condemnation in the believer's heart whenever he yields to the flesh; a conscious sense of darkening within, as though a cloud had passed between him and God, and shut out the light from the innermost chamber of his soul. The flesh is just such a veil between the believer and the conscious presence of God, and every time he walks in it he hangs up that veil. It is this very knowledge that these relapses into the flesh bring the hiding of God's countenance, which begets in the believer that watchfulness to die daily, to put off the old man, to press closer and closer to the side of Christ, that is so emphasized by Paul as the final condition of the blessed life. Not that such an act done in the flesh, such a relapse into the flesh-walk, costs him his soul. The question at issue here is not that of salvation by Christ, but of communion with Christ. The son who has yielded to an act of disobedience does not lose his sonship. But there is strain, and grief, and broken communion, in the home-circle. Sonship is as sure as the blood of Christ and the omnipotent hand-grasp of the Father can, make it. But communion with God is like the face of a delicate mirror; even the breath

THE SECRET OF HIS CONSTANT MANIFESTATION 95

of the flesh-life on it will condense cloud enough to shadow the outshining presence. How foolish then for a child of God to rely upon any past "experience," or manifestation of the Spirit, when he sees that the first step he may take in the flesh will cloud that manifestation! And how needful that he should press on to learn that final secret of abiding in Christ, which alone can teach him how these "breaks" in communion shall become fewer and fewer, until at last he has learned to walk in the Spirit, and reaches the glad consumation, where "the law of the spirit of life in Christ Jesus hath made me free from the law of sin and death."

Nothing within the pages of God's Word gives more helpful teaching concerning the truths of the Holy Spirit than the portion on the Vine and the Branches. It is not only marvelously clear, and simple, but comprises the whole of the threefold secret of the Spirit. Picture a branch grafted into the vine, in the springtime. As soon as the union is complete, the branch receives the life of the vine, which begins to pulsate through it. This illustrates the believer's receiving the Holy Spirit, through union with Christ by faith, at the time of his conversion. Suppose now some obstruction in the channels of the branch, which checked the flow of sap, so that although the branch had received, yet it was not filled. The moment this is removed the branch is filled with the life of the vine. This pictures the believer who has in truth received the Holy Ghost, but, by an unyielded will and life, is surely hindering the fullness of that life which he has as surely received. As soon as he gives himself wholly to God, he is filled with the Spirit already received. Here he too often halts. He tries to live upon a past experience. But the branch does not, yea, dare not. For it is not enough that the branch received the sap of the vine at grafting; or that it was filled with it the day it wholly yielded itself to it. But, every day and hour of its existence, it must continue to draw, moment by moment, upon the life of its nourishing vine. It must not only draw on that vine for birth, and bud, but for leaf, fiber, wood, bloom, and final fruitage. It must abide in the vine. It dare not rely today on yesterday's fullness. It dare not draw on the vine one day, and fail to draw on it the next. If it did, then, when the vintage came, there would be no fruit. It must abide in the vine. The application to the believer is evident. He must learn this final secret. For "As the branch cannot bear fruit of itself except it abide in the vine; no more can ye except ye abide in Me."

3. *The nature of Abiding.* And now what is it to abide in Christ? Exactly what does Christ mean, when He uses these words to describe the final secret of the Holy Ghost? How shall we abide in Him that we may know the joy of His promise—"and I in you"? If the climax of the Christian life is reached here—as it assuredly is—how important it is for us

THE SECRET OF HIS CONSTANT MANIFESTATION 97

to have not vague, and indefinite notions, but clear and well-defined knowledge of just what is meant by this term. Men, it is true, have written beautiful essays on abiding; religious poetry is full of descriptions of it; rich and beautiful thoughts have been uttered concerning it. Yet somehow they have all been vague, shadowy, and mystic, in the face of our earnest desire to know just what abiding is, that we may practically incarnate its supremely important truth into our own every day lives. The difficulty here, as always, is that we seek men's thoughts, instead of God's thoughts, about the truth. We ignore the greatest rule of Bible study, namely: when we come upon a phrase of unknown meaning let us ask God, who wrote the Book, what *He* means by it, instead of seeking man's opinion about it. That is, concerning some obscurity in one part of the Word, seek to find some other portion of that Word which clears it up. How much we have slighted God's Word, in this respect, is well illustrated by the very term we are considering. For all the while men have been groping, and spiritualizing, and theorizing concerning the beautiful truth of abiding, there has been staring in our very faces God's own definition of it, as clear, simple, and practical as He alone could make it. We find it in I John 3:24, R.V.: "And he that keepeth His commandments abideth in Him and He in him." How strange that we have so long missed it! It is the same simple truth as that of manifestation (John 14:21). And why? Because it is a question not of salvation but of communion. It affects not our safety but our walk in Christ. Failure to believe in Christ costs us our souls; but failure to abide in Him, after belief, costs us our conscious communion with Him, veils the manifestation of His presence. Abiding expresses in a single word the conditions of Manifestation, treated in a previous chapter. For, to "him that keepeth my commandments I will manifest myself" (John 14:21); but "he that keepeth my commandments abideth in me" (I John 3:24); therefore "it is to him that abideth that I manifest myself." The logic of this is clear. *Abiding is thus the constant keeping of His commandments, in response to which He manifests Himself in constant communion with His children.*

But some one says: "If my abiding in Christ depends upon my keeping the multitude of commandment in His Word, then I can never reach it, for I cannot even remember them all, much less keep them, and so must despair of ever learning this final secret of the Holy Spirit." Not so, beloved. Turn again to His Word in I John 3:23: "And this is His commandment, that we should believe on the name of His Son Jesus Christ, and love one another, as He gave us commandment." To us, who are under grace, all the commandments are fulfilled in this great twofold commandment of Faith and Love; "faith working through love." So important a truth have we now reached that it merits all the prayerful consideration we are capable of giving it, in the

THE SECRET OF HIS CONSTANT MANIFESTATION

two remaining sections, and to it alone we shall, in conclusion, yield their full limits.

Abiding in Faith

We have seen that Christ manifests Himself, through the Holy Spirit, to Him who does His will, that is, to him that keepeth His commandments. We have seen also that the constant keeping of His commandments is what He calls abiding in Him, and that it brings not His incoming, or indwelling—both of which are already effected in the believer—but that constant revelation of Himself through the Spirit, for which every believing heart longs. We have seen, too, that all these commandments, whose keeping constitutes the Abiding Life, are embodied in the great twofold commandment of Faith and Love. We take up at this point, then, the Faith side of the Abiding Life; the first half of the great commandment of I John 3:23, the continual keeping of which is to give us the final desire of our heart; is to constitute that abiding in Him which brings His abiding in us.

What then is this faith which comprises so integral and important a part of the Abiding Life? Does it differ from the faith through which we are justified, through which we receive forgiveness of sins, and the gift of the Holy Spirit? If so, how? We answer that its essence is the essence of all faith, a looking to Jesus. But it is not so much difference from, but enlargement upon, our first knowledge of faith. It is a constant looking to Jesus for the continuous manifestation of the Spirit; even as, at the beginning, it was an act of looking to Jesus for the incoming of that Spirit. To make plain this thought, let us notice two points:

First. The believer in himself is spiritually dead. "In me, (that is in my flesh,) dwelleth no good thing." "For ye are dead, and your life is hid with Christ in God." The believer has thus no spiritual life in himself, apart from Christ Jesus. He has physical life, soul-life, but no divine life, apart from Christ. The simple fact of the new birth is a crushing proof of this. So hopeless is this spiritual deadness within that there must be a new birth. His old life cannot be reformed, or improved, or in any way utilized by God. There is no process, even of divine alchemy, by which the base metal of "the flesh" can be transformed into the fine gold of "the Spirit." He must be *born again*, born of *God*, born *anew*, born *from above*, born *of the Spirit*. The life which comes into him then is a new life; it is not his own, but the life *of God* in him. He is not a flesh-improved man, but a God-indwelt man. It is not that he has a better old life than the sinner possesses, but another *new* life, which the sinner does not possess at all. He is not called upon to try to amend, but to put off the "old man." God has the same sentence for the old life in him as in the sinner, namely, condemnation.

Second. Jesus Christ is spiritual life. "I am the way, the truth, and the life." "When Christ, who is your life, shall appear." "God hath given us eternal life, and this life is in His Son. He that hath the Son hath life; and he that hath not the Son of God hath not life." "In him was life"; "I am that bread of life"; "I give unto them eternal life." Thus, though the believer is spiritually dead in himself, yet Christ is spiritual life. And the believer receives life, not as a gift apart from Christ, but by the gift of Christ. Jesus Christ does not so much impart life as He inbrings life. That is, spiritual life comes to the believing one by the incoming of Christ, who is life. Thus the spiritual life in the believer is not his own; it is Christ dwelling in him. The believer never receives a gift of spiritual life which is now his own possession, independent of, and separate from Christ; he receives Christ Himself to indwell in the power of the Spirit.

Therefore the believer is portrayed as a man in himself spiritually dead, indwelt through the Spirit by Jesus Christ, who is his spiritual life. That old nature is just as dead a thing in the believer after conversion as it was before. It must be regarded as utterly worthless. Its carnal mind is "death," is "enmity with God," and in no way subject to God or susceptible of spiritual improvement in the believer, any more than in the sinner. Hence the believer's only hope is to give up his own self-life, as utterly hopeless, and begin to look solely to the Christ-life within him. He whose nature is sinful can look only to Him who is sinless; he who is weakness must look to Him who is strength; he who is empty must look to Him who is all fullness; he who is dead must look to Him who is life. So his new life must not be improved "I" but it is "no longer I that live, but Christ liveth in me: and that life which I now live in the flesh I live in faith" (Gal. 2:20, R. V.). Paul finds out that he is not only justified by faith, but that "the just shall live by faith," not only that he has received the Spirit, but that he must walk in the Spirit. He has reached the broadest conception of faith the believer can grasp, in reaching the faith through which we are not only born of God, but the faith through which we live in God—the faith of abiding. What then is this Faith? It is that habitual attitude by which one who, in himself is spiritually dead, is constantly looking to, and daily and hourly drawing upon, the life of another—the fullness of life of Jesus Christ within him. This is the life of faith; this is the walk of the Spirit; this abiding, on the Faith side of it. Of Faith in this broad sweep of the term the Word of God has much to say, and seems never weary of emphasizing its supreme importance. "After the same manner in which ye have received Christ Jesus, so walk ye in Him," is one of

THE SECRET OF HIS CONSTANT MANIFESTATION 103

the truths which Paul seeks most earnestly to press upon his hearers. And how did we thus receive Him? Was it not by ceasing from all self-righteous works of our own? Was it not by coming, in despair, to the end of self-effort, and self-justification, and throwing ourselves, in most helpless trust upon Jesus Christ, and upon Him alone? Could we, by any possible effort of our own, accomplish forgiveness of sins, and reconciliation with God? Could we blot out a single stain of the multitude that crimsoned our sinful lives? Nay; for "without shedding of blood there is no remission of sins," wherefore we had, perforce, to cast ourselves, in utter helpless faith, upon Jesus Christ to accomplish that which we could not possibly compass ourselves. It was thus that we received Christ Jesus. Now after the same manner we are to walk in Him. But a walk is simply a reiterated step. Wherefore, just as we took the first step of helpless faith in Christ alone for the receiving of the Spirit, so must we take each step in our walk, our life with Him, for the constant manifestation of that Spirit. Do we desire power? We must look to Him for it each time it is needed. Do we long for love? We must look to Him for His, for ours is cold and selfish. Do we desire anointing for service? We must look to Him renewedly, at each recurrence of such service. Do we need guidance, wisdom, tact, gentleness, longsuffering, peace, joy? We must look to Him for it all. Note this same truth beneath the surface of Romans 6:4: "That like as Christ was raised from the dead by the glory of the Father, even so we also should walk in newness of life." The statement is here made that our Christian walk in the new life should be like as Christ was raised from the dead. Can we conceive of a more perfect picture of helplessness than a dead man? Christ was, as to the body, dead. That dead body could not of itself rise, move, breathe, or stir; it was in itself utterly powerless. Hour after hour passed and it lay in the tomb, in the grasp of death, with no power in itself to rise, but awaiting the touch of God the Father. Then came the mighty quickening of the resurrection, by which "God raised Him from the dead." Christ did not raise Himself; it was not so appointed; He was raised by another—the Father. Now in this same manner is the believer to walk in the new life. He is to realize himself as dead, and helpless, and is to be daily and hourly looking to, and depending upon another, even Jesus Christ, even the Holy Spirit within, for every step of his walk "in newness of life," even as he did for the first step into the same. Beloved, do we realize that our walk in the Spirit is to be a constant, momentary life of faith, as surely as our salvation was by an act of faith? That we must not only be regenerated by faith, but live by faith? Do we believe that Christ meant exactly this when He said, "Apart from Me ye can do nothing"? Dare we lead that meeting; write that paper or letter; make that address; hand out that tract; speak to that soul about Christ; make that decision; take

THE SECRET OF HIS CONSTANT MANIFESTATION 105

that next step—dare we do anything without that swift uplift of faith to Him in whom alone dwelleth spiritual life? Have we incarnated this fact of our own insufficiency into our every day Christian walk? Do we realize that this is not simply a theme for religious essays, or a rather mystic subject for prayer-meeting talks, but is meant to be the most intensely practical truth Christ can give to us, and to be inwrought into every act, every word, every thought? Are we constantly looking to the indwelling of Christ? That self is worthy of all distrust, and Christ worthy of all trust, we know. But are we living it? Has "Apart from Me ye can do nothing" become a part of our life as of our creed? "It is the Spirit that quickeneth [maketh alive], the flesh profiteth nothing." Only the Spirit can make alive; only the Spirit can beget men and women from the dead. Words spoken, prayers uttered, acts done in the energy of self alone, have no power of spiritual germination. If this is true, how many of our works are "dead works"? Except the Spirit speak through us, pray through us, work through us, there will be no quickening in those about us. The sermon delivered in pride of intellect, or rush of mere human eloquence, may excite the intellect, arouse admiration or stir emotion, but it cannot transmit life. And naught but life begets life, for "It is the Spirit that quickeneth." "I do not often have to reproach myself for failure to serve, but I do often for serving without anointing," said a noted Christian worker. Ministry without the Spirit, of what value is it? The answer is ever the same: "the flesh profiteth nothing," and proves how solemn is our responsibility to live the abiding life; the life of constant distrust of self, and constant dependence upon, and drawing from, the indwelling Spirit.

The necessity of such an abiding life may be illustrated in an object-lesson of every-day observation. There are two systems of running electric cars today. By one, power is laid up in storage batteries, of amount sufficient to run the cars a definite number of hours, or miles. Such batteries, when once charged, become for the while independent sources of power and light, and the car is itself a potential self-propelling agent, needing no aid from without. But there is another, the trolley system, which differs wholly from the first named. In this the car is a dead, helpless thing, with no power whatever of self-propulsion. But above it runs the slender copper cable thrilling with the life that constantly pulsates through it from the distant power-house. The instant the helpless car reaches up and touches that overhead current, it becomes instinct with life, power, and motion. Now, it is not its own life and power, but another's, and the moment it ceases to touch upon the "live" wire, that moment it becomes the same helpless, motionless mass. Its continuance in the place of power depends wholly upon its constancy of contact. The lesson is obvious. Even so must the

THE SECRET OF HIS CONSTANT MANIFESTATION

children of God keep in constant, momentary, unceasing touch with Jesus Christ, if they would know the continuous manifestation of the Holy Spirit. For God does not fill them on the storage-battery, but on the trolley principle. He does not charge them with independent power, but unites them in dependent faith to Jesus Christ who is so charged. It is Christ (Acts 2:33) who received of the Father the promise of the Holy Ghost; and it is Christ who "hath poured forth this which ye see and hear." It is by virtue of our union with Christ, then, that we have received the gift of the Holy Ghost. And it is only as we abide in Him; as we press closer and closer to Him; as we daily draw our life from Him by communion and prayer, and continuous looking to Him, that we know the constant manifestation of the Spirit. God thus does not fill us as we might fill a pail, with a supply independent of, and separate from, the fountain. He fills us as the branch is filled from the vine, by union with it, and daily, hourly, drawing upon it, for every whit of its supply. And so he who looks to Jesus constantly will not lack blessings and baptisms, but he who looks to blessings and baptisms will often lose hold upon Jesus. The Lord wills to keep us in this place of dependence. He will not so fill us with the Spirit as that we may run for a year, a month, or a day alone. To do so would be to make us independent of Christ; fill us with self-reliance; puff us up with pride; shatter faith, the very foundation of the abiding life; and wreck our life of fruit-bearing in Him. Nay, beloved, our spiritual life is not our own, but drawn from another. Self-dependence means barrenness; Christ-dependence brings fullness. "Ye are dead and your life is hid with Christ in God."

Note well here that this abiding is not a term of standing, but of state. It does not precede salvation, it presumes it. A man in Christ has the Spirit in virtue of his union; but many a man in Christ loses the manifestation of the Spirit through failure of communion. Many a Christian is right in standing, but wrong in state; sure of salvation, but slack in walk, and communion. In such, barrenness of life and powerlessness in service indicate not lost salvation in Christ, but lost fellowship with Christ; not lost justification, but lost manifestation; not loss of saving faith, but loss of abiding faith in the sense already used.

The simple thought then of this faith of abiding is that of a constant looking to Jesus for our spiritual life. These three words, looking to Jesus, picture perfectly the posture of the soul that is abiding in Christ. The moon keeps looking to the sun, for every gleam of her reflected radiance; the branch keeps looking to the vine, for every whit of its life and fruitage; the drinking fountain keeps looking to the supplying reservoir, for every drop of water it is to pour out to its thirsting visitors; the arc light keeps

THE SECRET OF HIS CONSTANT MANIFESTATION 109

looking to the great dynamo, for every ray of the stream of light with which it floods the midnight darkness. Even so the child of God who would master the final secret of the Holy Ghost, the secret of His constant manifestation, must keep looking to Jesus, moment by moment, until such abiding in faith becomes the constant attitude of his soul. It may be, yea, it will be difficult, at first. To incarnate this principle of looking to Christ alone in every detail of our lives means much to us all. To silence the clamor of fleshly voices; to lean not upon the fleshly understanding; to quell the energy of fleshly haste; to distrust all plans not born in or from prayer; to lay the hand of strong restraint upon every impulse, until it has been proved, by prayerful waiting, to be of God; to not only say "no confidence" in the flesh, but to live "no confidence" is an attitude not attained with ease, and at a single bound. But it shall be ours; Jesus has commanded it (John 15:4), and all His commands are enabling. And as out of our very failures to abide, the deep need of abiding becomes more manifest, we shall, even as we look to Him for the power to abide, come at length to it. And then, really accepting and practicing our own helplessness, to look to Jesus for strength and find it; to look to Him for guidance, and see with our own eyes the wondrous ways in which He leads; to look to Him for anointing, and to be as conscious of the Spirit's gracious presence as we are of our own identity; to look to Him for fruit-bearing, and be astonished at the fruitage He can bear through such branches as we are—how precious is all this fruitage of abiding life!

Beloved, are we so dissatisfied with self as to feel the supreme need of Christ alone? Do we realize that in ourselves we are dead men and women? The very fact that a man must be born again, do we realize this to be in itself the most tremendous indictment against, and proof of the utter worthlessness of our own natural Self-life, that a holy God could ever array against us? Have we accepted the logical consequences of regeneration, in their bearing on holy living? Do we realize our need of living in God, as well as being born of God? Are we conscious of our need of Abiding? Are we "following after," abiding? Surely its reward is rich, for He Himself hath said, "abide in Me and I in you"!

ABIDING IN LOVE

We have seen the truth of abiding, on the Faith side of it. We have seen how the believer must keep on looking to Christ, day by day, for his spiritual life; must keep in constant hourly, touch with Him; must by a life of prayer, communion, and trust keep momentarily drawing upon Him "in whom dwelleth all the fullness of the Godhead bodily." But, as we have seen, "he that keepeth His commandments," he it is that abideth in Him. Abiding is the keeping of His commandments. There is more than one. There is not only "believing in the name of His Son Jesus

THE SECRET OF HIS CONSTANT MANIFESTATION

Christ," but "love one another"; not only Faith but Love. Hence abiding is not only communion, but ministry; not only inflow, but outflow; not only an attitude toward God, but also toward men; not only looking to Jesus, but loving others. He, therefore, who would live the abiding life in all its fullness and symmetry, and know the manifestation of Christ which attaches to it, needs not only to be constantly drawing by faith upon the fullness of Jesus, for His daily walk and life, but needs also to be constantly loving others instead of loving self. That the abiding manifestation of the Spirit of God can be only to those who not only live the life of faith, but the life of constant love, is founded on the very nature of God, for

1. God who is love—love of others—can manifest Himself only to those who are also willing to love others. God is Love. We see Him as Love in the declaration of His Word. "God is Love and he that dwelleth in love dwelleth in God." "He that loveth not, knoweth not God." "I have loved thee with an everlasting love." "Having loved His own, He loved them unto the end." "As the Father hath loved Me, even so have I loved you." "God so loved the world that He gave His only begotten Son." We see it in God the Father, planning from the eternal ages for the salvation of men. We see it in God the Son, as He poured out His life in unwearying ministry for the souls and bodies of men; as His heart agonized

in compassion for the multitudes, like sheep without a shepherd; as He endured with majestic patience the taunts and gibes of the judgment scene; as He bowed in agony under the bloody blows of the scourge; as, at the last, in His own body bearing our sins on the tree, His dying breath was spent in plaintive prayer for His murderers. We see, too, God the Spirit to be Love. How tender in pleading with men! How gentle in rebuke! How tireless and patient under resistance! How loath to leave, though flouted and scorned! How quick to forgive the crimson sins and remorseful follies of the vanished years of a wasted life! Yea, the Father, who gave His only begotten, to send salvation; the Son, who bled upon a felon's cross to bring salvation; and the Spirit, who for thousands of years, has yearned over, and wrought with men to apply salvation—these three are one God of eternal, self-sacrificing, changeless, quenchless Love—Love of others.

Hence the very nature of God, which is Love—love of others—requires for its manifestation a life which is willing to love as He loves—love not self, but others. The only way to secure the manifestation of the electric current, is to supply the steel, or copper wire, or other conductor which its nature demands. Even so, the only way to secure an abiding manifestation of God in us is to supply the conductor which His nature demands, in a life which is yielded forever to love others even as He loves. The

THE SECRET OF HIS CONSTANT MANIFESTATION 113

life of a child of God, so yielded to live out the great command "Love one another," is as much a conductor for the manifestation of the God of Love, as the metal wire is for the manifestation of electric force. For this is the law of the Spirit's activity; it is the only line along which He will operate. Who would expect that Spirit to manifest Himself through a murderous, or a sensual, life? Neither can He manifest Himself through a life whose ruling principle is love of self, for He is utterly unselfish. Therefore, when Jesus Christ states clearly that the manifestation of God is to "him who keepeth His commandments," and then says, "This is my commandment, that ye love one another even as I have loved you," He makes the manifestation of God in the Spirit a logical necessity to him who is willing to shift the center of his life from love of self, to love of others, and a logical impossibility to him who is not willing so to do.

2. Hence that child of God will have the fullest manifestation of God in the Spirit, who adopts as the deliberate purpose and principle of his life, *The love of others* instead of *the love of self*. This is the law through which the Spirit acts, and if he would have the manifestation of that Spirit he must deliberately accept this law as the law of his new life. True, this law of love is the exact opposite of the law that all his lifetime has been controlling him. But that is the very point. He needs a different law

of action ("a *new* commandment I give unto you") because he is now yielding himself to a different life, a new life, the life of the Spirit. And so when Christ gives us a new nature, He gives us a new commandment. When He gives us a new life, He gives us a new law of manifestation adapted to that life. And since the new nature is the deadly foe and the exact opposite of the old, we would expect that the law of its manifestation would be the exact opposite of the law of the old. Hence the believer who desires the manifestation of the Spirit must expect for the government and regulation of his new life a new principle, totally different from that which has shaped almost every act of his past life; the principle of loving others instead of loving Self. And what a far-reaching, heart-searching, breathtaking change this is! To cease to grasp all, and begin to give all; to cease to seek all, and begin to surrender all; to cease accenting "take care of number one," and begin to accent "let every man care for the things of others"; to no longer seek the high place, but the lowly one; to aim now to minister, instead of to be ministered unto; to no longer seek, but to shun the praise of men; to no longer save the life, but lose it for others; to no longer lay up, enjoy, and be at ease, but to suffer, and spend and be spent for Christ Himself—all this is a complete reversal of the deep-rooted, all-controlling principle of the natural human heart, the principle of self-love. To the world the mere suggestion of such a thing is

THE SECRET OF HIS CONSTANT MANIFESTATION 115

astounding! That a man should deliberately renounce all self-seeking; self-praise; renounce his gaining, grasping, dreaming, striving, toiling and scheming for self; and as deliberately give himself to seek, strive, toil, suffer, sacrifice, plan, plead, pray, and live for others—this is something the natural man will not receive. It is monstrous, impracticable, incredible, suicidal! But, beloved, this is exactly what Jesus Christ did, and exactly what you and I must do to know the manifestation of His life within us. As surely as love of self is the first law of nature, is love of others the first law of God. Astonishing, sweeping, and destructive of every self-interest as the law of Love is, yet he who yields will know God as he never otherwise can know Him. He will be most filled with the New Life who yields most fully to the New Commandment. This New Commandment is the supreme expression of God's will for our earthly walk. Who so yields to it reverses the motive principle of his being. But he also reverses the whole current of manifestation. He who once knew the self-life in its fullness, comes to know, as never before, the fullness of the Christ-life.

3. He, who would know the abiding manifestation of God, needs to *abide* in Love. We need not only to accept this great commandment as the rule of our life, but need to carry it into our daily life in actual practice. The act of surrender to do God's will of Love is not enough, unless it is followed by

a daily, hourly doing of that greatest command. And the manifestation of His presence and love, which accompanies surrender, will fail of continuousness, if we do not daily live that which we yield ourselves to live—the love-life of God. Hence, the need of abiding in Love. For "he that abideth in love, abideth in God, and God abideth in him" (I John 4:16, R. V.). To abide in Love is to incarnate the great law of Love of others into every detail of our daily life. Not only must the self-life be renounced, by a solemn definite act but the habit of selfishness must be replaced by the habit of Love. We are to practice the new commandment in everything, "following after Love," as Paul says, until it becomes the steadfast law of our being, in all its details. We are to make "Love one another" the touchstone by which to test every thought, word, and deed of our daily lives, until all are brought into conformity to the law which was supreme in the life of Jesus Christ Himself. The rebuke you administered yesterday to a brother in Christ, was it done in love, or vexation? The counsel you gave, was it proffered in love, or pride of opinion? The meeting you led, the address you made, were they in love—to help others—or to add to your own reputation? The money you gave, was it in love to the lost—or in pride, and self-esteem? The remarks you make about others, are they in love? The thoughts you cherish in your secret heart concerning them—are they, too, full of love? Your giving, spending, ministering; your pray-

THE SECRET OF HIS CONSTANT MANIFESTATION 117

ing, and purposing, are they all in love? This is the supreme test of every detail of your life, by which you may know whether it is "God that worketh in you," or Self. And how quickly that abiding in love becomes a condition of the manifestation of the Spirit! Let a day be spent in this attitude of love to others, instead of love of Self. Let the words be kind and gentle; the acts helpful, unselfish, and considerate; the hours filled with loving, unselfish ministry; and the heart the abode of sympathetic, kindly thought. That day is a day of blessing, and the consciousness of the Spirit's blessed presence in the heart. But let the words be harsh; the thoughts envious or spiteful; the acts selfish; the hours filled with self-seeking instead of self-forgetfullness; and who does not know the conscious shadowing of God's presence, the conscious grieving of the Spirit in such days and hours? In the grain elevators of the West are different compartments for the various grains. Open one spout, and the golden corn manifests itself in a rich outflowing stream. Open another, leading to a different chamber, and the amber wheat pours forth in like unceasing stream. Open others, and the oats, or barley, or rye will severally flow forth according as the respective channels to each are tapped. Now, within us dwell the Spirit and the flesh; the God-nature which is Love, and the old nature, which is selfish. The moment we do an act, speak a word, think a thought in love, God, who is Love, manifests Himself. But the moment we speak in harshness, act in selfishness, and think in envy, hatred, or spite, the Flesh manifests itself. The law is as certain, simple, and inexorable as the law by which the kind of grain manifested depends upon the specific channel which is thrown open. If we yield to Love; will to love; incarnate Love; abide in Love, we shall surely be blessed with the conscious manifestation of the God who is Love, for we have opened the channel through which the Spirit of Love is bound to flow forth. But if our words are bitter; our thoughts and our aims constantly centered in self; our actions purely selfish; our lives self-centered, and loveless, then the manifestation of the Flesh, the self-life, the old nature is just as certain and inevitable as the manifestation of the Spirit to him who walks in love. Christ cannot manifest Himself through a life of murder or theft, that is self evident. But is it equally evident to us that Christ cannot manifest Himself through any act that is selfish or *un-Christ-like?* Every root of bitterness, every yielding to selfishness, every harsh judgment in our daily walk must, and does of necessity, break Christ's communion with us. How zealous and careful should we be then to abide in love! Let every act be done in love to others. Shun a selfish act as you would a sensual one. Shrink from an unloving thought or suggestion as you would from the hiss of a serpent. Eschew hasty bitter words as you would poisoned darts or daggers. Realize—what so astounds the natural

THE SECRET OF HIS CONSTANT MANIFESTATION 119

heart—that God loves, regardless of His treatment by others—"He is kind to the unthankful and the evil"—even so should we. So, if some grievous wrong, insult, or unkindness goads you from your attitude of love, justify it not, but hasten to confess, and find forgiveness from Him who prayed for those who murdered Him, as well as for those who loved Him.

Note well here that the supreme expression of love is ministry, even unto sacrifice and death. Love is not mere sentiment; mere emotional outflow. True, it must first be in the heart, whose attitude is to be steadily one of love for others. But thence it flows forth in ministry, in service, in sacrifice for others. "Little children let us love in deed and in truth," says John. "Hereby perceive we the love of God because He laid down His life for us." God so loved that He gave, He served, He died, for the lost world. This is the test of Love. The inevitable outcome of the love-life within, is ministry and service without. True love must minister; the love of Christ constrains it so to do. Yet be it remembered that they who lie upon beds of suffering and helplessness, may in the secret outgoings of their hearts, and in the ministry of prayer for others, live the love-life as truly as those who minister by hand, tongue, or pen. For as in giving, so it is here, that "if there be first a willing mind, it is accepted, according to that a man hath and not according to that he hath not."

4. Faith is the gateway of communion with God; Love the gateway of ministry to men. He who keeps them both constantly open has learned to abide in Christ. The believer is the temple of the Holy Ghost. That temple is double-gated. Faith is the gateway open Godward; Love is the gateway open manward. Through Faith the divine life, so to speak, flows in to us; through Love it flows out to others. Faith is the channel of communion with God; Love the channel of ministry to men. God desires not only to pour His life into us through Faith, but through us to others, through Love. The Spirit not only wants us to let Him in, but also to let Him out to others. It is not enough for us simply to receive the Holy Spirit. It is not enough to have Him indwelling in us. It is not enough to have His love, peace, and power in ourselves, and for ourselves only. There is some one else in the universe besides God, the giver of the Holy Spirit, and us, the recipients. There is an unsaved, dying, perishing world, whom He loves even as He loved us. Unless they see Christ through us, they will never see Him; unless they hear of Him through us, they will die in darkness; unless He touches them through us, they will never know the touch of His life and power. When He walked the earth He was constantly pouring out His own love-life in sacrifice, ministry, and blessing

THE SECRET OF HIS CONSTANT MANIFESTATION 121

to all about Him. Now, He is "no longer in the world," but we are in the world as members of His body, branches of Him, the living Vine, and He longs to continue pouring forth that life through us. Faith is thus the channel of divine inflow; Love the channel of divine outflow. Through Faith God has all chance to work in us; through Love all opportunity to work through us. "Faith which worketh through Love," is the way Paul puts it. Faith looking hourly to Jesus, constantly receiving His inpouring life, as constantly pours it out through Love, the door kept open toward the perishing. He abides in Christ who keeps both these doors constantly open. Neither dares to be shut. To close the door of faith is to have the inner man grow weak for lack of communion; to close the door of love is to have him grow weak for lack of ministry. Thus the believer is a channel for the Spirit who is, in figure, a stream, "Out of him shall flow rivers of living water . . . this spake He of the Spirit which they . . . should receive" (John 7:38). That which has been received is to flow out. A good channel is always receiving, always full, and always outflowing. To be a good channel one needs to keep constantly open at the point of inflow, and the point of outflow. Therefore these two gateways of Faith and Love must be kept constantly open. Through Faith, the gateway open Godward, as it were, we constantly receive the divine life in communion. Through Love, the gateway, opens manward, we constantly give out the divine life in ministry and service. The channel which shuts one gate, ceases to be a channel. For inflow without outflow means stagnation; and outflow without inflow means emptiness. We dare not cease from Faith; we dare not relax in Love. We must pass from the inflow of communion to the outflow of service; and back again from the outgiving of service to the replenishment of communion. He who shuts either the gate of communion or the gate of ministry, writes over his life, "No thoroughfare"; but he has no sooner done this than the Spirit, with invisible hand, writes over that same life, "No abiding."

Not realizing that both are needed to form a rounded, symmetrical, complete life in Christ, men have tried to divorce them; essayed to live one without the other. Realizing that apart from Christ they could do nothing; seeing the need of close, constant communion with Him; conscious of the blessing, and power of the life of prayer, they have given themselves wholly to the Faith side of the abiding life. They have retired from the world with its sin and follies; they have hidden themselves in the seclusion of cell and cloister; they have given themselves to prayer, meditation and communion. But when God revealed Himself to them through the life of communion, instead of opening the door of Love, applying themselves to ministry and giving out spiritual blessing and life to those in need, they

THE SECRET OF HIS CONSTANT MANIFESTATION 123

essayed to keep to themselves the Life which is given for all men. Thence came the morbid, unnatural, unhealthful type of life that dwelt in the monastery, and the hermit's cell, and degenerated, when unaccompanied by the every day ministry of love, into spiritual death and barrenness. Christ Himself could not live such a life, but when "annointed by the Holy Ghost, He went about doing good." The Faith side of the abiding life is absolutely essential. We must realize our own spiritual deadness; we must look to Jesus constantly; we must, hour by hour, draw upon His divine life. But "Faith without works is dead"; inflow without outflow is stagnation; communion without ministry is one-sidedness.

Others there are who give themselves wholly to Christian service and activities. Their life is one continual round of meetings, societies, conventions, addresses, and servces, without number. To them hours of prayers are an unknown factor; communion is a meaningless term; waiting on God a waste of precious time; the guidance of the Spirit and the life of trust are sound without significance. Yet these lives, with all their "busyness," lack a radical something. There is fret and fume; worry and anxiety; conscious lack of quickening power in service; absence of joy, peace, and blessing in the lives they are living with such intensity. It is but the same shield viewed from the obverse side. Works wrought in our own might are dead works; the chamber of prayer is the only true powerhouse; ministry, without anointing, is lifeless; we must touch Christ before we touch men; we can not pour out, if we have not received from Him. One touch of a live wire will thrill a man through and through, but you may touch him all day with a dead one and never quicken him. Faith without ministry is dead; ministry without faith—which is ministry apart from Christ—is declared by Christ Himself to be nothing. He then who continuously lives out these two great commandments of Christ; He who constantly keeps open these two doors of Faith and Love; he who thus becomes the thoroughfare of the Holy Spirit—has learned the final secret of the Spirit—the secret of the abiding life.

Wherefore, to abide in Christ is to live a life of constant faith Christ-ward, and constant love man-ward.

Beloved, have we learned this final secret of the Holy Ghost? Are we living the abiding life? Do we realize, on the one hand our helpless, hourly dependence upon Jesus Christ as the only fullness of life for us? Are we learning the lesson of looking to Him in all things? Has it become the habitual attitude of our lives? Are we slow to speak, to plan, to act, until we have been in touch and counsel with Him? Are we not only pouring out our lives for Him, but—what is still more important—are we holding ourselves in such an attitude that He can pour out His life through us? In short, are we remaining, staying, living, abiding, in faith? Furthermore do we realize that He is Love—Love of others? That He wants us to be like Him and therefore says, "A new commandment I give unto you that ye love one another even as I have loved you"? Have we given up our Self-love then, and made it the supreme purpose of our lives to love others? And, if so, are we living it? Are we asking ourselves day by day and hour after hour: "Did I do this in love of others; did I plan this in love; did I speak this in love; did I give, or minister or serve in love; love of others?" Do we throttle every harsh word, resent every selfish thought, refuse every selfish act because each violates the great love-law of our new life? Do we understand that this Love means practical, constant, life-long ministry and service for others, even as He served when on earth? Are we keeping both commandments continuously? Are both gates open? Are our quiet hours given to communion? And our busy ones to ministering in Love, however humble and commonplace the things we do may seem? Are we so constantly looking to Him, and so busy in loving others that we are beginning to understand, just a little, that wonderful sentence "It is no longer I that live, but Christ that liveth in me"? Have we thus tasted of abiding? Are we following after abiding? If so let us rejoice. For it is not only ours in promise, and ours in command, but it is to be ours in actual, conscious experience, as

His own blessed Word declares: *"And hereby* WE KNOW *that* HE ABIDETH *in us* BY THE SPIRIT *which He hath given us."*